FROM PREP

Through the Eyes of an NFL Mom

Donna Stallworth

authorHOUSE®

AuthorHouse™
1663 Liberty Drive
Bloomington, IN 47403
www.authorhouse.com
Phone: 1-800-839-8640

Published by AuthorHouse 1/11/2013

ISBN: 978-1-4670-7620-3 (e)
ISBN: 978-1-4670-7621-0 (sc)

Library of Congress Control Number: 2011960934

Dedication

 This book is dedicated to the memory of my cousin Bobby Cornell Forbes

Bobby was like my Lil brother/ son. He meant so much to me. Bobby knew how important education was. After all, he was a graduate of Clemson University. You could see how important it was by his dedication to helping his sons with their homework. You saw it when he was encouraging his nieces, nephews, cousins and friends. Although Bobby loved sports he was always reminding them that school came first and sports second.

Bobby read my first book titled "From Prep to Pro" Through the eyes of an NFL Mom, and he was looking forward to reading my second and third books.

He always said to me that the books were great and that I was doing a great job getting that information out there to parents and students because it was much needed. He was proud of me. He was always encouraging me and asking me if I worked on my books today?

We were always talking about football in our conversations on a regular bases. I will miss hearing his voice on the other end of the phone. I will never forget that special hug he gave me the night before he passed away. He will be missed by us all.

We all Love you dearly Bobby. R.I.P.

To my grand children: Ke'shaun, Kiana, Nadyca, Larnyz, Londyn and Devaughn whom I love very much. You are all my blessings from God. I am very proud of all of you and all that you've accomplished. You all have done well in school. Continue to stay focused on school and always do the best you can in all that you do. Keep your hearts and minds focused on college, getting a good education and earning a degree.

Ke'shaun, you are the oldest grand child and you are headed to college. You have made some tremendous accomplishments and have done very well. I am very proud of you. Stay focused with your school work. I know you love sports and have done a great job in every sport you've taken on. It's very important to earn that degree so that you will have something to fall back on. If you keep God in your heart and on your mind everything else will fall into place.

Make sure you read the books. You will learn some things.

I love you all dearly. Be Blessed!

This book is also dedicated to Parents, guardians, students, athletes, coaches, and anyone with an interest in leading our youths, encouraging them, and motivating them to further their education.

Acknowledgements

I first give all the glory, all the honor and all the praise to God for the gifts and talents that he's given me. I know that if it had not been for the Lord, I would not have written this book. Thank you Lord for Blessing me.

To my children Larry Jr., Jamara, Donte' and JJ. for your encouragement, love and support. Anything I needed help with you were there to help me. My children know the love and passion I have to write books and that this is just the beginning of many more books to come.

To my cousin Bobby Forbes for always encouraging me to write my books and always asking me if I worked on my book today. I wish you were here to see the completion of the books.

To Rhonda Knight, you have been an encourager and an inspiration to me. Thank you for the suggestions you gave me, for everything you did to help me re-write these books, the prayers you prayed for me and the love and support you gave me. I learned a lot from you about the business as an author and a business woman.

Felicia Young, I want to thank you for all the prayers you prayed for me, and the suggestions and ideas you gave me. You've been an inspiration to me. You showed me a lot of things that you've done with your own business as an author that has helped me with my book and business and I thank you for that. You were patient with me and said for me to call you anytime, which I did.

Nina Archie for researching different things for me and being supportive to me and encouraging me.

Deanna Moore thank you for the encouragement, motivation and homework assignments you gave me to help me with my 'Prep to Pro speaking engagements. Thank you for all the support you showed me and everything you've shared with me to become a successful business woman. Most importantly, being on tour for your "I Think I Am Foundation" has given me a lot of exposure, so I really thank you for that.

Dr. Sirretta Williams, you have encouraged me, motivated me, and inspired me to do more in the business world. I've learned a lot from you. I've seen a lot of work that you've done on your own and I've watched you work day in and day out, yet you still took time out to talk to me, explain things to me and pray for me. Thank you.

To my two new quiet friends, Sheryl Howard and Lisa Randolph. You two ladies didn't want to talk much on camera during our tour, but I really enjoyed hanging out with you both as well as getting to know you. Both of you ladies have a lot of good information to share so don't be shy. Thank you for your kind words of encouragement and prayers.

Christina Lee, thank you for always calling and checking on me, encouraging me, believing in me, praying for me and doing whatever you can to help me fulfill my dreams and visions. Thank you for helping me with different ways to promote my books, and using your marketing skills so that others will learn of me.

To Mr. L. Martin and the Asante Award Committee for believing in me and recognizing that the information in my book was deserving of my receiving an Asante award. Receiving that award encouraged me to re-write the book, put more information in it, which allowed me to turn the previous one book into two books.

To Bea Bailey for all the help and information she so kindly and willingly gave me as she too is an author.

Jeffrey Wilson, thank you for believing in me, inspiring me, and supporting me. For going out of your way to tell others about my book and encouraging them to buy it and read it. I also want to thank you for believing in making Prep to Pro come to light and becoming successful.

I want to thank my neighbor Peggy for helping me with the last minute problems I had with my computer programs. I couldn't have completed my books without your help. You and Kurt have always been very supportive to me and I thank you and appreciate you.

Last but not least, to my family members for all the love they continuously give and the support they always show me, my church family, my Pastor Dr. Ephriam Williams for all of his words of wisdom and his teachings through the word of God. To my many friends who are always willing and ready to support me.

To all of you I say "Thank you".

I really would like to thank the teams that I worked closely with at Authorhouse to make this book into what it is today.

Tim Murphy was the representative I spoke with when I first called Authorhouse to inquire about their services. He was so patient and answered all of my many questions. He took time to explained the process and the steps I would take to get the book published. *Faith Allen* was my check-in coordinator. She was patient, kind and a hard worker. We worked diligently together. *J.R. Turner* was my Design consultant and he was very patient and kind. He didn't rush me with anything. He explained things to me before we proceeded to the next step. He made sure that we both understood each other before we moved onto the next step. I thought it was great when he congratulated me on the completion of the book. *Teri Watkins was also* with the design team. She too was very helpful and she made sure that I had the right forms and explained them carefully to me. *Greg O'Connor* was the marketing consultant and he gave me great tips about marketing. *Ryann Jacoby,* thank you for helping with issues/problems we ran into and overseeing them, while doing your best at trying solve them. Last but not least I'd like to thank the book consultants for helping with the completion of my book. So again to you all I say "Thank you".

Hearing the words "Congratulations" confirmed to me that I had once again made another great accomplishment in my life. God gets the glory for it all!

A Message from the Author

I wrote a book titled *FROM PREP TO PRO! Through the Eyes of an NFL Mom.* As I was writing this book I wondered how many children or students I could help. I wondered how many parents I could encourage to be more supportive to their children. I thought about my own children. I talked to them about college at an early age. I taught them how to set goals and make plans for their lives. I wanted the very best for my own children and I want the very best for yours. So I thought about using a Mother's voice to speak to other children by writing books. I wanted the book to be easy to read and understand. I wanted to encourage the youths, the parents, guardians, and anyone who cares about the success of our children the way that I do. I want our children to be successful.

That's when I wrote my first book which I won an Asante Award for. Asante means thank you.

During one of my motivational speaking engagement sessions, I gave parents and students an opportunity to ask questions. While listening to the students, I realized that some of them wanted to know more about attending college, while a few others wanted to know more about the recruiting process for athletes. The parents had a lot of questions and a lot of them stated that a lot of the information that was in my book was very helpful. Some of them stated that they had no idea of how certain things worked . That's when I realized that I needed to re-write my first book and add more information to it.

Some of my speaking engagements were pertaining to the first portion of the book "FROM PREP" while other speaking engagements were geared towards the second part of the book "To PRO". Therefore, I decided to separate the one book and make two books out of it because I was speaking to two separate audiences. I decided on "FROM PREP" Through the Eyes of an NFL Mom for part 1 and part 2 would be titled TO PRO! Through the Eyes of an NFL Mom.

The "FROM PREP" book is not just for athletes, but for any student. Also for parents and for anyone with a desire to support, motivate and encourage our youths to attend college.

This book can be used as a guide or a tool for both the parent and student. A playbook journal is included in the book. I teach the student how to set goals and plan for their future. I offer parents and students information regarding college, scholarships, the recruiting process for the athlete, and a lot more topics.

After you read this book, you will realize that my guidance, motivation, and inspiration makes this book a must read guide for students, athletes, and families.

It is my desire that if part one helped you or someone you know, then you will be inspired to read part two.

Donna Stallworth

Forewords

Reading the book truly helped prepare my family and I for the life that we where about to be entering into. With my brother and I both making the transition from high school to the NFL at the same time, things got crazy, emotional, and moved extremely fast, but fortunately this book served as a handbook to help slow things down and make sense of it all.

It's a quick read and has great application pages. I recommend that whoever is going through this process or intending on it, definetly read this book.

Chris Carter
OLB Pittsburg Steelers

The book From Prep was a huge help to my husband David and I. We have been blessed with 2 sons that were drafted into the NFL in the 2011 draft. When they were being recruited both in the same year for college we had no idea what to expect and had to learn as we went. It was a blessing to be able to use your book as a guide through the NFL draft process. It helped us to interview the many agents that sought after our sons by  giving a detailed list of questions to ask and specific warning signs to look for. One of our sons read the book and said he benefitted from it greatly. Although we were completing the college phase of their careers when the book was published I would encourage any parent that has a child who is serious about sports to use the book as a manual to guide them through the process that will hopefully take he/she as far as they want to go.

Thank You,
La Genia Carter

Sons: David Carter Arizona Cardinals
Chris Carter Pittsburgh Steelers

As parents, one of the things we want for our children are lives better than ours. We know that our children's gifts are of God and that it is our obligation to see that these gifts are fully developed. With this in mind, all of the choices/decisions made regarding "the next step" are thoroughly scrutinized, prayed upon, over pondered, and second guessed.

This book has provided an impetus for students, athletes and their parents transitioning to their next level. Questions are being answered and guidelines are suggested which can be individualized to one's situation.

This information serves as a reference, "GPS" or a blueprint of sorts in preparation for, and while experiencing the actual transition from the beginning to the rank of professional. The sequences discussed in the book have not waivered, therefore, having this resource can be likened to having a friend hold your hand and walk with you through life's altering processes. It gives you enough insight to know when red flags should go up and when/what things happen next.

After reading the books, not only were we able to assist our son in the collegiate decisions but we were also empowered enough to assist him as he began his career in the NFL.

Cudos, Donna for arming us with the pertinent information to achieve success.

Barry & Ophelia M. Shaw
Parents of Jarrod Shaw Cleveland Browns

From Prep is a must read book, especially if you want to be an athlete or pursue your dreams. Donna has allowed her experiences in being a woman of God to become a fantastic mother, because she loved and nurtured her children into great successes and through this book showed how ambitious she really is.

This book will help you to have faith in your dream and to pursue it by having an education and a Plan B. She never gave up. It should tell moms and dads to search out your children's gifts and talents and start seeking God about His plans for them and begin to dream. Everything she said in this great book  is true. It pretty much tells how God equipped us to be where we are today. Thanks Donna. Great Job in sharing! It is very helpful. God Bless you on your journey or the dream that God gave to you.

Ms. Felicia Young,
The mother of Vincent Young, Jr. #10 QB NFL

The book "From Prep" is an awesome book and it is very well written. Upon my reading it, I realized that the Author had extraordinary insight of the process needed for preparation to be acclimated into the world of professional sports and articulated her expertise in a way that was conducive for a young person pursuing their passion and dream regarding sports. Furthermore, Donna Blueford Stallworth shows us how to be a supportive parent as well as what are the intelligent moves one most make to assure success and she also designed the book to encourage youth to be an intricate and active part of that process.

As a mother of five daughters who were not very athletic, I had very little knowledge of sports other than sometimes being a spectator, however I, yes even I could follow and understand the procedures necessary to advance further in this pursuit. As a matter of fact what I learned from "From Prep" I was able to share with others who have children with aspirations of an athletic career. It matters not what the sport is, football, basketball, baseball, track etc., or what gender your child is, male or female therefore, if you follow the formatting listed to the tee, you as a parent or even supportive relative or friend, more than likely will be looking in the face of that child who will be a professional athlete in the very near future.

Lastly, as I was reading this book, I saw visions of just how far this book and the second book "To Pro" would go and how effective they would be, uplifting and inspiring youths and parents alike. I saw auditoriums filled with people listening to the wisdom Donna possesses, happy, eager faces on looking with visions of hope. This woman is so passionate about the success of your child or children and it is evident in her writing. Congratulations on your purchase of this book, you and your child are destined for the purposes God has already ordained for you. My only suggestion is to also purchase "To Pro" and have the upper hand in the "game".

Evangelist Rhonda Knight,
International Author and Motivational Speaker

It's a great book!!! I think students should be required to read & study this book. It's very informative and the information is clear! If I would have read this book prior to going to high school, I know for a fact it would have had a major impact on how I selected the school to attend, as well as what I should have been looking for in a good college or university.

More importantly, it would have helped my parents, who knew nothing about the NCAA!!

Mike Mckenzie
Retired New Orleans Saints Cornerback

A Letter from Donna's Children

It is a great feeling being children of a very strong, prayerful and powerful woman like our Mother.

"*From Prep* " will serve as a guide for high school and collegiate students and student athletes who are trying to further their careers and make it to the next level. I urge all parents out there who are serious about their students/athletes' future to immerse yourselves in this step-by-step guide. This book will help you to learn all of the ins and outs of the journey from prep to pro....

I wish to congratulate Mom. You are the GREATEST for keeping your heart and mind on the futures of all student athletes. This will no doubt be a great guide for all parents and students to follow for many years to come!

Your son,
Larry

Mommy, what a wonderful accomplishment to have written your 1st and now 2nd and 3rd books. It has been your goal and dream for years. Just like your book is a teaching tool, you always taught us to go with our dreams and visions. You went with your dreams and visions. You never let anything or anyone get in your way.

You have always been a very loving and supporting Mother, who educated and loved her children.

As an adult I can still say "God has truly blessed me when he gave me to you.

Your Loving daughter
Jamara

We are proud of our Mother for sharing some of her very special parenting skills by way of this book. Our Mother has always told us that she was going to write books after she retired; no surprise to us at all, she is continuing on writing her second and third book.

As with her first book, this book "From Prep" shows our Mother's love, passion, and most of all her ambition to help other parents make good decisions about their children's future.

This book will be a good guideline not only for parents of young athletes, but all children and students who have dreams about their future.

I urge you to pick up copies of this book "From Prep" Through the Eyes of an NFL Mom for your Jr. High School students, high school students, college students, libraries, camps etc.

Thanks Mom for not only trying to be a Mom and an encourager to other students but for encouraging me and loving me unconditionally.

Your 2nd son
Donte' #19 NFL WR

Although the books 'From Prep to Pro" and "From Prep" was not published when I was entering my college career, all of the information from the books were already known by my Mother so her knowledge was a great help to me, knowing what to look for in college including school information like recruiting, scholarships , what to expect when I do go to college, warning signs/ things to look out for and many more topics. You just have to buy the book to see.

This book has a "Gold Mine" of information for all parents of students, college students, and athletes who wish to get more information regarding colleges, scholarships, the recruiting process and much more information. Also for students and athletes who want information to help them get the best opportunity for college success.

Now that I have finished college, and have gone "From Prep", I am planning my next journey "To Pro" which is the title of the 2nd part of this book. I have gained a lot of knowledge from this book, so I urge you to pick up a copy or copies of both books.

Thanks Mom for all the knowledge and encouragement you've always given me and for all the love you've always shown me.

Your son
Je'von (J.J)

Mother, we congratulate you and we love you very much. We wish you luck in the future with the many more books we are sure you will write as a guideline for parents and students.

With love,
Your children

Contents

DREAMS AND VISIONS XXXV

PART 1: FROM PREP 1

SUCCESS STARTS AT HOME 3

RESPECT AND DISCIPLINE 3

"D" IS NOT FOR DUMMY 4

PROACTIVE PARENTING 6

STAY INFORMED 8

DONNA'S GRADE CHART 9

ATTITUDES 10

CHALLENGES 11

PEER PRESSURE 12

COMMUNICATION 13

BULLYING 14

CHILD MOLESTATION 18

HAZING 22

YOUR FORMULA FOR SUCCESS 27

A PLAN AND A GOAL 27

PLAN B 28

SETTING GOALS 29

SEVEN SIGNS OF SUCCESSFUL PEOPLE 30

PREPARING FOR COLLEGE 33

TESTING: ACT VS. SAT: 36

    ACT 36

    SAT 36

    ABOUT THE SAT SCORES 37

    UNDERSTANDING THE SAT SCORES 37

    SAT II 38

NCAA 39

NCAA ELIGIBILITY CENTER 40

COURSE REQUIREMENTS 41

    DIVISION I ELIGIBILITY: 42

    DIVISION II ELIGIBILITY: 42

THE IMPORTANCE OF ATTENDING COLLEGE 44

REASONS WHY SOME STUDENTS GO TO COLLEGE....... 46

EXCUSES FOR NOT ATTENDING COLLEGE 47

FAMILIARIZE YOURSELF WITH COMMUNITY
COLLEGES VS. STATE/UNIVERSITY COLLEGES 48

BEING RECRUITED *51*

THE RECRUITING PERIOD 51

SELF PROMOTION 53

LETTER OF INTEREST.. 54

PLAYER PROFILE 55

DON'T FAKE THE NUMBERS....................................... 56

THINGS TO CONSIDER 57

NCAA RECRUITING RULES SUMMARY 57

    NCAA ELIGIBILITY CENTER 57

    CORRESPONDENCE 57

    PHONE CALLS 58

    CONTACTS 58

    OFFICIAL VISIT 58

    UNOFFICIAL VISIT 59

    EVALUATIONS 59

VISITS/COLLEGE OPEN HOUSE DATES........................ 60

INFORMATION TO GATHER.. 61

IF YOU INTEND TO PLAY SPORTS 62

QUESTIONS TO ASK A COACH DURING YOUR VISIT..... 62

QUESTIONS NOT TO ASK A COACH DURING YOUR
VISIT 63

MY EXPERIENCE 64

YOUR POSITION 66

SCHOLARSHIPS.. 66

FULLY FUNDED 67

VERBAL COMMITMENT... 68

NLI (NATIONAL LETTER OF INTENT)........................ 70

TO THE PARENTS/GUARDIANS................................ 71

COLLEGE STUDENT ATHLETE...................................... *73*

ON YOUR OWN 73

NEW TECHNOLOGY 75

ROOMMATES 75

CHOOSING YOUR CLASSES 77

NCAA ELIGIBILITY REGULATIONS............................. 79

KNOW THE NCAA RULES 81

ADDITIONAL NCAA RULES FOR THE UPCOMING YEARS (2012-2015) 86

    STIPEND PAYMENTS 86

    MULTIYEAR SCHOLARSHIP................................... 87

    STRICTER STANDARDS FOR HIGH SCHOOL STUDENTS AND FOR JUNIOR COLLEGE STUDENT TRANFERS.................................... 88

    POST SEASON RULES 88

    BASKETBALL RECRUITING 90

REDSHIRTING 93

MEDICAL REDSHIRT 94

GRAYSHIRT 94

REDSHIRT FRESHMAN 95

TRUE FRESHMAN 95

TRAVELING WITH THE TEAM 96

DISAPPOINTMENTS.. 97

TRANSFERRING... 98

CHOOSING TO LEAVE SCHOOL EARLY 99

CONCLUSION *101*

PART 2: PLAYBOOK 103

Introduction

Dreams and Visions

As a little kid, were you ever asked the question, "What would you like to be when you GROW UP?" You may have replied a doctor, nurse, policeman, fireman, scientist, teacher, singer, dancer, a mom or a dad. Have you ever envisioned, or even dreamed of being a professional athlete? Have you ever imagined that you played in the NFL or NBA? What about becoming a DOCTOR, or a NURSE? Hold on to your dream. Keep your vision alive. You can become anything you set your heart and mind to be. You can make that dream a reality, but there's a CATCH! You have to work hard to get it and you have to stay focused.

Nothing is just handed to you on a silver platter. You have to work at it, physically and mentally. See yourself furthering your education, getting your degree, being a professional athlete or anything you want to be. Remember that dreams do come true, so DREAM BIG.

Visualize yourself doing what you would like to do or have always wanted to do.

When you have a vision, you should write it down to help you stay focused on it. You'll know you are getting closer to your dream when you want it so badly you can SEE it, and you can FEEL it. Sometimes it will seem so close that you can even TOUCH it. You might be so excited about it you get anxious. You get excited because you're happy that your day is finally here. When your dreams are getting closer to reality, that's how you will feel.

♡ WHAT ARE YOUR DREAMS AND VISIONS?

Note: Whenever you see the icon, ♡ you are reading a question from the Prep to Pro Playbook (Student Athlete Journal) that's located in the last chapter of the book. You can either use the journal at these times, or merely give the question some thought to prep your mind for when you do begin to use this effective tool.

Part 1:
FROM PREP

Chapter 1

Success Starts at Home

RESPECT AND DISCIPLINE

In every household a child should have rules to abide by and chores to do. This teaches responsibility and the ability to follow directions at an early age. When a child starts school, they will know how to follow directions when teachers tell them what to do. Hopefully, they are responsible enough to get their homework done and turned in at the appropriate time. There will be rules in the classroom to follow and to abide by. If a child has had rules at home they will less likely have an attitude when given instructions. Teachers are not babysitters. They are there to TEACH, and children are there to LEARN!!!

The same applies when playing sports. Children have to be taught discipline at an early age so they will know how to be respectful, follow directions and obey rules. If you would like to participate in sports while in high school, you have to keep your grades in good standing. You have to attend school on a daily basis and pay attention in class so that you can increase your learning skills. All of these things require discipline and respect, for yourself and others.

"D" IS NOT FOR DUMMY

Your grades will be monitored starting with 9th grade reports. It's IMPORTANT at that time that you maintain a "C" grade or higher for each class. A "D" grade won't get you into a state college or university and when applying for a scholarship it is UNACCEPTABLE!!!

If you do get a "D" as a final semester grade, it does not mean that you are a dummy, and don't ever let anyone tell you that. Just consider it a DUMB DECISION, and strive to do better. If you are having a difficult time with a particular subject and your parents and friends cannot help you, stay after class and get help from your teacher. Let the teacher know you want to get a good grade and that you are interested in learning. Most teachers are willing to help a student who is willing to learn. Try not to have a bad attitude towards your teachers. The reason most teachers are in the classroom in the first place is because they like teaching and they want to help further their students' educations.

If you find that a teacher is not willing to work with you, then you don't need to be in their class. Speak with your school counselor or advisor to resolve that issue. If a teacher gives you a grade you feel you don't deserve, talk to them and work it out. Stay after class if you have to. If you cheat in class you are only hurting yourself. Don't wait until the last moment to get help. You know when your grades are slipping, so get help early. There is nothing wrong with finding a tutor and doing extra credit work if possible. You must put in TIME and EFFORT, whether you are in the classroom or participating in sports.

Parents, you need to know what's going on with your child. Even if that means taking time out of your schedule and taking a seat in some of their classrooms. Attend "BACK TO SCHOOL NIGHT," and ask to see the grade book. Meet all the teachers, get to know office staff, the principle, the vice principle, and even the hall monitors. Yes, the hall monitors, because they see what's going on every day. Talk to your child's counselor. Make sure they're taking the correct courses to attend college. You are responsible for your child. It should be important to you how well your child does in school. Everything that concerns your child should concern you. If not, you will see the end result.

PROACTIVE PARENTING

It's one thing to say it, but as parents, we have to act to help our children do the right thing. I know we all have our own schedules and you can't be everywhere all of the time, but you have to do the BEST you can and pick your moments to step in. I always wanted to make sure that while my children were attending school they were being respectful to their teachers and making it to class on time, even if that meant visiting the classroom on a regular basis.

On one memorable occasion, I received a phone call from the school informing me that my oldest son was regularly late for a particular class. I couldn't figure out how that was possible when the class he had before was right next door. So I decided to pay a visit to the classroom. I put on my son's pants, shirt, and hat. I wore some sunglasses and drove to the school. Just before the bell rang, at the time of day he was suppose to leave one class and show up to the class he had been late for, I took a seat in his desk and waited.

Other students filed into the class and took their seats and while I was waiting and watching the door, I saw my son in the hall. He walked right past the classroom and me with a young lady at his side. He didn't even see me! I waited in his seat, in his classroom until he showed up late! Upon his late arrival to class, he realized someone was in his seat. Since I was disguised it took him a few seconds to realize that "someone" was his mom. I gave him THE LOOK, and asked his teacher if she was going to use her chalk board. Her reply was no, so

I asked her if my son and I could borrow it for a few minutes. Neither she, nor my son or his classmates knew what was about to transpire.

In front of the class I made my son write on the chalk board 100 times that he WOULD NOT BE LATE FOR CLASS AGAIN. Then I asked him to apologize to his teacher for disrupting the class. From that point on he was never late for any of his classes ever again. By the way, he was a senior in high school and he never forgot that his mom would check up on him… and neither did his two younger brothers and little sister.

STAY INFORMED

In most schools, students have to pass a proficiency examination and an exit examination before graduation. Make sure you double check with your child's counselor to make certain all graduation requirements are met in a timely manner.. Remember that the final grades for each semester from 9th grade through 12th grade must be a "C" or better. You can also help your child by simply telling them that you love them and showing them that you care by keeping track of their grades, visiting their classroom and helping them with homework.

If your child participates in sports, please go to the games and meet their coaches. Don't just drop them off and pick them up when the practice or game is over. Trust me, even if they don't show it now, your child will thank you later.

Be SUPPORTIVE. If a child knows that their parents care, they will do their best in all that they do. They will feel good about themselves and will want you to be proud of them.

DONNA'S GRADE CHART

Remember...

A = **A**WESOME

B = **B**E CAREFUL

C = **C**AN DO BETTER

D = **D**OES NOT MEAN DUMMY

♡ DO YOU NEED TO BRING YOUR GRADES UP? IF SO, HOW WILL YOU DO IT?

1. TRY HARDER?

2. REPEAT THE CLASS?

3. DO EXTRA CREDIT?

4. HOW ABOUT SUMMER SCHOOL?

5. FIND OUT IF AFTER SCHOOL CLASSES ARE OFFERED?

ATTITUDES

Your attitude has a lot to do with how much you can accomplish. At some point you will have to answer to someone, whether it is your parent, guardian, teacher, coach or your employer. **Your attitude can either work for you or against you.** You can have a bad attitude when:

- Fighting
- Throwing things
- Using bad language
- Wanting to argue all the time
- Having negative thoughts or jealousy
- You are not willing to listen to someone who is trying to help you

DON'T BE ARROGANT. A good positive attitude will take you far. This can also apply to parents because they too need to have good attitudes to set good examples for their children. You may have seen parents embarrass their children by being rude and disrespectful to them and to others. We as parents have to be role models for them. We want our children to honor us. Some children don't respect their parents because their parents don't respect them. Support your children and respect your children. It means so much to them.

♡ Do You Have Attitudes That Need Adjusting?

Parents, Do You Need To Make Adjustments To Help Your Child?

CHALLENGES

There will always be challenges for you in some way, shape, form or fashion. Whether it's with another student, your grades, your teacher, your parents, your family members, your church family or your friends. There are good challenges that you give yourself to improve in a positive way. Challenges like striving to do better in school, being a better friend or listening to your parents. Trying out for a sport or singing in the choir may be good challenges.

There can also be bad challenges that are negative obstacles to overcome. Dealing with bad attitudes, jealousy, envy, or even physical attacks can be "bad" challenges. Dealing with these challenges present a test to your positivity and good attitude. It's possible to turn any challenge into a positive for your life. Overcoming obstacles will help make you mentally tough and also show you who your true friends are.

You can even be a challenge to yourself by thinking you are "ALL THAT" and don't need to work hard or to practice at all. You might even think that you "GOT IT LIKE THAT!!!" You might feel that you don't have to listen to coaches, teachers, parents or even your friends. Well, think again, because **you don't know everything**. There's always something to learn so keep an open mind and allow yourself to grow.

♡ WHAT DO YOU SEE AS YOUR GOOD CHALLENGES?

♡ WHAT DO YOU SEE AS YOUR BAD CHALLENGES?

PEER PRESSURE

At some point you will encounter peer pressure, envy, and jealousy. Hurtful things may be said about you or a family member to discourage you. I have seen some students give other students such a hard time that they were no longer motivated, only to see the perpetrator advance. Such individuals want others to fail because they have failed themselves or don't have anything positive going on in their lives. They may even want to take someone else's position.

Peer pressure can cause you to do things you normally would not do. DON'T LET OTHERS PROVOKE YOU TO DO WRONG OR TO SAY THINGS YOU SHOULDN'T SAY. Learn to take the HIGH ROAD and don't stoop to their level. You are better than what they are trying to make you out to be. It's best to be yourself, even when that's not easy to do.

♡ What Peer Pressures Do You Face?

COMMUNICATION

One of the biggest keys to a positive attitude and overcoming challenges is COMMUNICATION. Learn how to communicate. Open your mouth and talk. Talk to your parents, family members, coaches, a counselor, a teacher or a friend. No one can read your mind. When you don't communicate it leaves others wondering, guessing and assuming what you want. Lack of communication can lead to frustration.

You need to communicate with your parents so that they can help you. Some kids don't think it's cool to let their parents know when something is bothering them. You'd be surprised, your parents may actually be a big help. If there is a problem at school and your parents are informed, they can talk with whomever they need to help solve the problem or offer you advice that may help.

Some people communicate through their actions when they get tired of speaking. Although action speaks louder than words, it is not always the best way to handle things. There is a time to speak and a time to act. COMMUNICATING in the RIGHT way at the RIGHT time is important.

BULLYING

Bullying is a widespread and serious problem that needs to be addressed and STOPPED! It is not just messing around or just a phase that kids go through because bullying can cause serious and lasting harm.

Bullying can be either emotional, verbal or physical abuse. It could also be done through email, face book, or twitter.

It is a behavior to intentionally hurt another person physically or mentally. It is also a behavior where an individual will act a certain way to gain power over someone. Believe it or not bullying can include name calling, teasing and even spreading rumors about you.

To sum it up, there are many forms of bullying.

VERBAL: name calling, teasing

SOCIAL: spreading rumors, leaving people out on purpose, breaking up a friendship

PHYSICAL: hitting, punching, shoving

CYBERBULLYING: using the internet, mobile phones, email, face book, or twitter to harm others.

Bullies will sometimes give up or get bored when they don't get a response from their target. In my opinion they give up or get bored because it's no fun for them if they don't get a response from the person they are trying to bully.

Bullying should be taken VERY SERIOUSLY, especially whenever a child or a student tells their teacher or parent that they are being bullied. This is another reason why I feel it is very important for parents to have a good relationship with their children. I also feel strongly that this is just another reason why I think parents should visit their child's classroom often to make sure that they are not being bullied. Visit them during recess time to just watch how they play and watch who they are playing with. Your child doesn't have to know that you are coming for a visit. You might have to check into the school office first but that's fine. It's even more important to make sure that YOUR child isn't the one being the bully.

If your child thinks or feels as though they are being bullied, you as a parent, family member, teacher, or a friend can help by listening to them. Teach them to ignore or walk away from that type of bully behavior. Teach them to talk to someone about the situation they feel they are in. Reassure them by letting them know that they can come to you and talk to you about anything. Always talk to them about school, their classmates, who they play with, who they don't play with and what their reason is for not playing with that one kid. It's also a good idea to know who your children hang out with. Know who their friends are and where they live. I always told my kids to never be afraid to talk to me about anything. I was always questioning them about their teachers, their friends, and anyone else they were around.

I use to always go to the schools and show up in each of my children's classrooms. I was not only watching my children, but other children to see how they were acting in the classroom. I was watching the teacher to see how they were interacting with the students including mine. Even when they were playing sports, I was watching. When they would go on field trips, I was watching because I was there with them most of the time.

Parents should set good examples for their children and be good role models for them. Parents should not bully people because if you are a bully how are you going to teach your child not to be one?

PARENTS: Teach your kids not to be a BULLY. Let them know that if they are a bully, there could be consequences for their actions. Teach them to keep their hands to themselves. Teach them to not hit push or shove another child. Teach them not to hurt or harm another child physically or mentally. Teach them not to use the internet or their cell phones to bully someone.

IF YOU FEEL YOU ARE BEING BULLIED, OR KNOW OF SOMEONE BEING BULLIED, PLEASE REPORT IT TO YOUR PARENT/PARENTS, TEACHER, SOMEONE YOU TRUST, OR SOMEONE IN AUTHORITY.

DO YOU FEEL LIKE YOU'VE BEEN BULLIED BY SOMEONE?

IF SO HOW WILL YOU HANDLE IT?

ARE YOU A BULLY?

IF YOU ARE A BULLY , WHAT IS YOUR REASON FOR BEING A BULLY?

WHAT CAN YOU DO TO BETTER YOURSELF TO NOT BE A BULLY?

CHILD MOLESTATION

Children are being molested everyday. It is estimated that at least two out of every ten girls and one out of every ten boys are sexually abused by the end of their 13th year of age. Sometimes it starts even at an earlier age like 5 or 6 years old. This is all so very sad to me.

Children who are sexually abused are usually abused by a family member or a close friend. Usually someone whom they trust and feel comfortable with.

Child molestation is also a subject or a topic that some parents don't like to talk about or discuss, but this is a very important issued that should be talked about and discussed with your children at an early age in your home. The reason I say "YOU" should talk to them at an early age in your home is so no one else can get to them and talk to them before you get a chance to and THEY tell YOUR CHILD that it's all right for THEM to touch them. In other words as an example, if the molester is a family member or a close friend, you don't want either of those people getting to your child first and making your child think that it's ok that they touch them on certain parts of their body when IT'S NOT OK TO DO THAT!

Sometimes the molester will tell the child that if they tell anyone they will deny it. They will sometimes tell the child that if they tell anyone, they will hurt the child's family. A lot of times these people won't mess with someone bigger than them. They mess with the little people. They are not always bold enough to mess with the big people.

My children know that I have always talked to them about not letting people touch them on certain parts of their body. I didn't even allow my daughter to sit on anyone's lap other than mine and her Dad's. I was always watching anyone and everyone who was around my children. My eyes were on them at all times. I believe in my heart that each and every one of them were able to read my eyes and know that my eyes were saying "I'M WATCHING YOU"! It really didn't matter whether you were a relative, a friend, a coach or a teacher. I didn't care. I was still watching you. And I still watch people. I even listen to what people say when they talk to kids. Again, "ALL EYES ON YOU". And that's how you should be with your children.

PARENTS: Teach your children at an early age about the parts of their bodies that no one should touch. Chest, buttocks, and genital area (private parts) are all areas that should be off limits.

Be on the watch if someone 5 years older than your child wants to hang around them all the time. Even if it's an adult and they are always wanting to hang around your child, stay alert of that. I'm not saying not to trust people, I'm just saying to keep your eyes open and watch. If someone touches them in the wrong area you want your child to be aware that it's not all right and it should be reported to someone.

I think some parents are too lenient with their children . They will let their children go over to someone's house without knowing anything about the child or the parents. They will let their children go places with people and not really know them. They will let their children roam the neighborhood or the streets and not know where they are. I just wish that parents would keep a closer eye on their children and know more about their whereabouts and who they hang out with. We just have to try to keep an eye on our children as much as we can.

Parents should talk to their children before anything happens. Let your child know that if something like that does happen, it's not their fault and they should report it to their parents or an adult they can trust. Let them know that it's nothing to be embarrassed about. Stress to them again how important it is to tell someone if they feel as though they've been molested. ALWAYS encourage your children to tell the truth. If they find themselves in a situation, make sure that they are telling the truth about everything that happened because it's important. Make absolutely sure that your child knows that if they are not telling the truth about something, there could be consequences.

Parents should just be careful about what family member, friend, teacher, or coach you let your child hang out with. Watch people at all times regardless of who they are.

IF YOU KNOW OF SOMEONE WHO IS BEING MOLESTED, OR WHO HAS BEEN MOLESTED YOU MUST REPORT IT TO SOMEONE.

IF YOU REPORT IT, MAKE ABSOLUTELY SURE THAT YOU ARE TELLING THE TRUTH AND NOT MAKING IT UP.

DO YOU THINK YOU'VE BEEN MOLESTED?

IS SOMEONE TRYING TO MOLEST YOU OR SOMEONE YOU KNOW?

IF SO, WHAT WILL YOU DO ABOUT IT?

DON'T BE AFRAID AND DON'T BE EMBARRASSED. IT'S NOT YOUR FAULT. BE HONEST AND TELL THE TRUTH.

HAZING

I've asked a number of students if they knew what hazing was and many of them did not know. A few of them including some adults said that they had never heard of the word before.

Hazing is an activity that's expected of someone when they join or participate in a group or an organization that might endanger, abuse or humiliate them. It can be an inappropriate behavior associated with the activities within an organization or a group.

If you choose to participate in an organization or a group make sure that you find out everything you can before joining. Find out if there is any hazing involved and if there is, what exactly does it involve. I'm pretty sure that if you want to join any type of group or organization, you've already spoken to someone who is already in the group or who has participated in some of the activities.

I think if anyone chooses to participate in hazing, it should ALWAYS be safe and not something that could hurt/harm another person. I would never want to be a participant in any activity that would require harming someone or even humiliating them and you shouldn't take part in it either.

Every single year you hear on the news or read in the newspaper of a student dying because of hazing. I've heard of anything from a student being forced or dared to drink heavily to taking what someone thought or was told was a harmless drug, or beaten badly, only to find out later that it caused someone's death. What parent wants to get a phone call from the police or the school saying that their child or student participated in this type of activity and either brought harm to someone or harmed themselves?

We can all help prevent hazing by looking and listening for signs of hazing. It doesn't matter if we are parents, family, friends, teachers, room mates, coaches, counselors, or advisors, we can all help in some way.

Pay attention to what you hear your child or another student talking about when it concerns hazing. Watch for behavior that is different, a change in personality, unexplained bruises, cutting, labeling, or shaving of body parts. Walking in groups or with groups. Performing certain task or requirements involving harming someone. Withdrawal from friends and family. There are so many things to look for. Some of these things that I mentioned may or may not be due to hazing but I would still question it if I had any concerns.

If you feel you or someone you know are being hazed after you've joined an organization or a group, you should not put up with it. You do not have to stay in it. You are not doing yourself or anyone else a favor by staying silent. Why would you even want to join or stay in a group or an organization that brings harm to another person? Get out while you can.

Instead of hazing activity being harmful, why can't groups or organizations turn it around and make it something positive. You can still find fun things to do instead of harmful things. THINK POSITIVE. THINK SAFE.

PARENTS IF YOU THINK YOUR CHILD IS IN ANY DANGER YOU SHOULD REPORT IT TO THE POLICE DEPARTMENT.

SIBLINGS, FRIENDS, ROOM MATES, TEACHERS, STAFF/FACULTY MEMBERS, COACHES, AND ADVISORS: YOU CAN ALL HELP TO PREVENT HAZING BY REPORTING ANY INAPPROPRIATE BEHAVIOR OR CONCERNS REGARDING HAZING. KEEP YOUR EYES OPEN AND LISTEN FOR ANY SIGNS OF HAZING. YOUR MAIN CONCERN IN THIS SITUATION SHOULD BE THE SAFETY AND WELL BEING OF THE STUDENT.

DO YOU BELIEVE YOU ARE IN A GROUP OR AN ORGANIZATION THAT INVOLVES HAZING?

ARE THE ACTIVITIES INVOLVED SOMETHING THAT COULD BRING HARM OR INJURY UPON ANOTHER?

IF SO WHAT DO YOU PLAN TO DO ABOUT IT?

DO YOU KNOW OF SOMEONE WHO IS INVOLVED IN HAZING ACTIVITY?

IF SO, HOW CAN YOU HELP THIS PERSON MAKE THIS ACTIVITY SAFE?

HOW CAN YOU HELP PREVENT HAZING FROM HAPPENING?

DO NOT PARTICIPATE IN HAZING ACTIVITY THAT IS UNSAFE.

ARE YOU INVOLVED IN ANY HAZING ACTIVITY?

IF YOU ARE INVOLVED IN ANY HAZING ACTIVITY, ARE YOU AWARE THAT IF SOMEONE GETS HURT, HARMED, OR INJURED IN ANYWAY YOU COULD BE IN TROUBLE BECAUSE OF YOUR INVOLVEMENT?

Chapter 2

Your Formula for Success

A PLAN AND A GOAL

Whatever you do, you must have a PLAN and a GOAL. Write it down. There are no right answers, but it's important that you know where you see yourself heading.

♡ PLANNING AHEAD:

- Where do you see yourself in the next 5 or 10 years?
- Have you looked ahead or are you just looking at tomorrow?
- Do you plan to attend college?
- If so, what would you like to accomplish?
- What do you need to do in high school to get to college?
- Do you want to go to college just to play sports?

- Do you want to play high school sports more than you want to get good grades?

PLAN B

You need to have a career to fall back on, just in case you don't succeed in the sports world. Regardless, a sports career will not last forever. Some athlete's careers last 20 years, while other's only last a few years… or less. You need a PLAN B. Work hard in the classroom and get the most from your educational opportunities.

You know the old saying, "Give 110%"? I thought that was funny, because I always gave 100%, and to give 110% means giving every ounce of strength you have and then some. Give just as much in the classroom as you do on the football field or the basketball court. Don't give 40% in the classroom and 60% on the field. Don't give 100% on the field and nothing in the classroom. To succeed you must give everything you have in all that you do. Nothing comes to you by just twiddling your thumbs. **Success says "I CAN", not "I CAN'T".** Think success. When things get hard in class, say "I CAN!" When you have to run extra at practice say, "I CAN!"

SETTING GOALS

Everyone should learn to set goals and to make plans. Those who don't set goals often keep searching and never find what they are searching for. Don't just settle for anything. THINK BIG, DREAM BIG, AND GET ORGANIZED. When we set goals and plans for our lives, we are motivated. It makes us feel good about ourselves and gives us something to look forward to. Goals and plans can help you get where you want to go. Whether your goal is to graduate from college or to play sports, you have to stay persistent, study hard and stay focused.. Set your goals, make a plan and a schedule and stick to it.

Some people may not set goals because they don't know how or they don't believe in DREAMS and VISIONS. They can't see themselves making their dream a reality or they are too lazy to take time to set goals. A lot of times people are afraid to set goals because they are afraid to "fail" by not reaching their goal. You are not failing when you try… you are only failing when you fail to try.

SEVEN SIGNS OF SUCCESSFUL PEOPLE

A PERSON WITH GOALS	VS.	*A PERSON WITHOUT GOALS*
• Will want to live life to the fullest		• Has no direction
• Will write it down on paper		• Every day is "Whatever"
• Knows what they want to be in 5-10 years		• Doesn't think about the future
• Wants to accomplish their goals		• Has no plans
• Is happy to see others succeed		• Critical of the successes of others
• Won't settle for less		• Will settle for whatever comes
• Can stay focused		• Can't stay focused

♡ TAKE A MOMENT AND WRITE DOWN YOUR GOALS.

YOUR GOALS MIGHT BE TO:

- Get better grades
- Take the proficiency exam and pass it
- Take the exit exam and pass it
- Do well in a chosen sport
- Graduate from high school
- Graduate from college with a degree
- Play a professional sport

If you don't have goals, you don't have direction. A PLAN is setting a goal. A GOAL is putting that plan into action.

EXERCISE:

Just in case you don't know where to begin or you don't know what your dreams are, take a few moments and try this exercise: **Go into a quiet room, close your eyes and visualize what you want to do in life. What would you like to be doing 5 years from now? 10 years from now? Wait a minute and keep your eyes closed. If closing your eyes doesn't work for you, or if it's not cool, then just sit in that quiet place and think for a minute. We're not done yet. Don't give up so easily. Concentrate until you can see it. OK, that's good. Now, did you see how easy that was? If you participated in this exercise, thank you. You did a GREAT JOB!**

♡ WHAT DID YOU SEE?

♡ HOW DID IT FEEL WHEN YOU WERE VISUALIZING YOUR FUTURE?

Write your script. Write your vision on paper. Why do this? If you write it down and you look at it all the time, it will help you stay focused. Writing it down also helps you persevere, stay encouraged and eventually reach your goals. You don't have to share your goals with everyone. You can keep them to yourself. Keep your eyes on the prize. The PRIZE is YOU and your ACCOMPLISHMENT.

The Mathematics of Success

GOALS	=	PLANS
PLAN	=	ACTION
ACTIONS	=	ACHIEVEMENT
ACHIEVEMENT	=	RESULTS
RESULTS	=	SATISFACTION
SATISFACTION	=	ME

♡ WRITE DOWN YOUR FORMULA FOR SUCCESS:

PICK ONE GOAL, THEN WRITE DOWN THE RESULT YOU WANT, THE PLAN/ACTIONS NECESSARY TO GET THAT RESULT AND THE SATISFACTION YOU WANT IN ACCOMPLISHING YOUR GOAL.

Chapter 3

Preparing for College

Why Is School Important?

You use school as an educational tool to obtain knowledge and skills.

You use the knowledge and skills you obtain from school to become:
- Independent and successful
- Get a good paying job/earn a good salary
- You'll have a better lifestyle
- You'll feel better about yourself

Students attend college for many reasons. For some, college might be a family requirement or expectation. Others may want to play sports or learn a trade.

♡ WHAT ARE YOUR REASONS FOR ATTENDING OR WANTING TO ATTEND COLLEGE?

Let this be the BEGINNING of your dreams. Imagine this as the starting point of the rest of your life, because what you do now will have a BIG impact on your destiny. So prepare well and make wise decisions.

Here are a few tips to help you prepare for college:

- Select a major. You won't have to DECLARE a major until you attend college. Find out what type of job you can obtain in that field.

- Meet with your counselor to make sure you are on track with your courses and grades.

- Search for colleges you may be interested in and decide which ones value your major.

- Visit the campuses of your choice. This is usually done with parents or guardians.

- Search for scholarships. There are many available. You just have to take time to find them.

- Take all required high school exams and pass them. Some of these can be taken before your senior year.

- Apply and take the ACT and/or the SAT tests. You do not have to wait until your senior year to take these tests.

- If you intend to play sports in college on an athletic scholarship, you will have to register with NCAA clearinghouse.

Some Websites for Reference

ACT*	Act.org Collegeboard.com
SAT and SAT II*	NCAAclearinghouse.net
NCAA Eligibility Center*	GovernmentGrants.com
Government Grants	ScholarshipWinnings.com
Scholarships	CollegeInfoScholarships.com
	FastWeb.com/Free-Scholarships

There are lot of scholarships available that you can apply for. You can go online and search for them. In my searching I was amazed at how many were available that I had never even heard of before.

Below you will find a list of a few of the different type of scholarships available to apply for:

Athletic Scholarships

Family Scholarships

Minority Scholarships

Subject Scholarships

College grants/Scholarships

Coca Cola Scholarships, Pepsi Cola Scholarships, Oprah Scholarships, Academic Scholarships, Dyslexia Scholarships, Nursing Scholarships, Fine Arts Scholarships, Law Scholarships, Native American Scholarships, Business PhD Scholarships, Lower Income Scholarships/Grants, United Negro Fund, Hispanic Scholarship, Burger King Scholarships, Ronald Mc Donald Scholarships, Accounting Scholarships, Medical Scholarships, PhD Law Scholarships, PhD Scholarships, President's Scholar, World Bank Scholarships

TESTING: ACT VS. SAT:

Most colleges accept both. It is wise to take both tests, then you're covered. Check with the college of your choice to find out their requirements. The ACT is accepted by most colleges and universities for admission. It has been described as easier in reading and grammar, but more difficult in math than the SAT. The SAT I is accepted as an admission requirement by almost all colleges and universities. If you are comfortable with writing and grammar, but haven't taken trigonometry, the SAT I may be the best test for you. SAT II, known as the SAT "Subject Test," is required in California and only a few other states. Again, make sure you check what the requirements are for the colleges you are interested in.

ACT

ACT (American College Testing) is an achievement test that measures what a student has learned. It covers four sections- English, Math, Reading and Science. It includes a science section, reading section, math section (7% includes trigonometry), grammar and punctuation and multiple choice. There is no "guessing penalty", which means there is no penalty for wrong answers. This test has 215 questions and lasts approximately 3 hours.

SAT

SAT (Scholastic Assessment Test) has 3 sections- Critical Reading, Math and Writing and includes a 25-minute essay test. It tests much more vocabulary than the ACT and becomes more difficult as the test progresses. The SAT has a "guessing penalty" which means a penalty is given for wrong answers. This 140 question test lasts for approximately three and a half hours.

ABOUT THE SAT SCORES

Colleges use SAT scores to determine whether or not you will be a good fit for their school. An SAT score can make you or break your application. In other words it can work for you or against you. The Sat scores are not the only thing colleges look at during the admission process. They may also consider essays, interviews, recommendations, community involvement and many more factors, but your chances of acceptance will increases with a high SAT score.

UNDERSTANDING THE SAT SCORES

There are three sections and three scores, each on a scale of 200-800.

Writing	(200-800)
Math	(200-800)
Critical Reading	(200-800)

An average score is approximately 1,538 points (Math 520, Writing 510, and Critical Reading 508).

An average total score is acceptable for most colleges and universities. Some of the top schools will expect you to achieve an SAT score of 2,100 or more.

A perfect score is 2,400 points.

PLEASE CHECK WITH THE COLLEGE OF YOUR CHOICE TO SEE WHAT SCORES THEY ACCEPT.

SAT II

SAT II or the SAT "Subject Test" tests individual subjects ranging from literature to Japanese. Every correct answer is worth 1 point, 0 is given for every omitted answer, and points are lost for incorrect answers. This test lasts for about 1 hour.

Before Taking A Test, Always Remember To Get Plenty Of Sleep And Eat A Healthy Breakfast. Take Your Photo Id, A #2 Pencil, A Calculator, And An Eraser. For Some Tests, An Admission Test Is Required. Always take the time to know what you are required to Bring To A Test And What You Are Allowed To Bring.

When you register to take the ACT or the SAT, you can mark the code 9999 so that the NCAA Clearinghouse will be one of the institutions receiving your scores. Remember that there will always be rules that you have to abide by- rules at home, rules in the classroom, rules to obtain a driver's license and rules for playing sports. If you don't abide by rules, there are consequences. So make sure that you, your parents, your coach and your counselor know what the NCAA rules are.

Learn to research anything that concerns you or anything you will be involved in. It doesn't take a genius to do this. You don't always have to wait for your counselor to tell you what classes you need to take, or how many credits you need. Keep track of these things yourself and stay ahead of the game. These are the actions of a responsible student and successful athlete.

When filling out applications, make sure they are neatly printed in ink or when possible, typed. Make copies of everything in case the school does not receive your paperwork or it is misplaced. Make sure all paperwork is sent in on time, BEFORE THE DEADLINE. Waiting to send it in at the last minute can be stressful. It's better to submit your application 2-3 weeks prior to the deadline, in case it gets lost in the mail. Even if you have applied for college stay on top of your grades or you may run into unnecessary stress or disappointment.

NCAA

The NCAA (also known as the National Collegiate Athletic Association or the NC Double-A) serves as the athletics governing body for more than 1,280 colleges and universities. It is an organization that determines whether athletes are eligible to play sports at NCAA institutions. The NCAA national office is located in Indianapolis. Member colleges and universities develop the rules and guidelines for athletic eligibility and athletic competition for each of the three NCAA divisions. The NCAA is committed to the student athlete and to governing competition in a fair, safe and sportsmanlike manner.

NCAA ELIGIBILITY CENTER

The NCAA Eligibility Center is located in Indianapolis, Indiana. It succeeds the current NCAA Initial-Eligibility Clearinghouse in Iowa City, Iowa. The eligibility center will certify the academic and amateur credentials of all college-bound student athletes who wish to compete in NCAA Division I or II athletics. There is no deadline to register, but you must be cleared by the NCAA Clearinghouse before you can receive an athletic scholarship. You will not need to file with the NCAA Clearinghouse for participation in NCAA Division III athletics.

Meeting NCAA admission requirements does not guarantee admission into college. It just determines whether students may participate in athletics during freshman year. You must follow each school's admission policy and apply directly to that school. Students can register as early as the beginning of their junior year, and if possible three to four months before enrolling into college. You can register online at the NCAA Clearinghouse website. If you received a waiver for the ACT or SAT then you are eligible for a fee waiver with the NCAA Clearinghouse. Students can get information from their high school counselor regarding the fee waivers or go to the NCAA Clearinghouse High School Administration page for information: EligibilityCenter.org

COURSE REQUIREMENTS

It is very important to work closely with your counselor to make sure that you are taking the correct number of core classes. Core classes are academic courses in one or more of these areas: English, mathematics, natural/physical science, social science, foreign language, non-doctrinal religion and philosophy.

What exactly is CORE COURSES?

Core Courses is the name the NCAA gives to high school courses that meet certain academic criteria specified by the association. Students must complete a certain number of core courses in order to be eligible to play for NCAA D1 (division I) and D2 (division II) sports.

Course Work Requirements for NCAA Athletics & NCAA Scholarships

The Mathematics of Success

DIVISION I

- 16 Core Courses
- 4 Years of English
- 3 Years of Math (algebra 1 or higher lever)
- 2 Years of Natural or Physical Science (including 1 year of lab science if offered)
- 1 Extra year of English, math, or science
- 2 Years of Social Science
- 4 Years of additional core courses (from any category above, or in a foreign language, non-doctrinal religion, or philosophy)

DIVISION II

- 14 Core Courses
- 3 Years of English
- 2 Years of Math (algebra 1 or higher level)
- 2 Extra years of English, math, or science
- 2 Years of Social Science
- 3 Years of additional core courses (from any category above, or in a foreign language, non-doctrinal religion, or philosophy)

Division I Eligibility:

- All students entering college must have completed 16 core courses in high school.

- Students with a minimum GPA of 2.0 after graduation must have either a combined SAT score of 1010 or sum ACT score of 860.

- There is a sliding scale between GPA and test scores: if a student has a high GPA, a lower test score is permitted.

Division II Eligibility:

- All students entering college must have completed 14 core courses in high school.

- Standards require a minimum GPA of 2.0 and a combined

- SAT score of 820 or sum ACT score of 68.

- There is no sliding scale for Division II.

Beginning on August 1, 2013 Division II will require 16 core courses (the same as for Division I).

WHY IS SCHOOL IMPORTANT?

IS SCHOOL IMPORTANT TO YOU? WHY OR WHY NOT?

THE IMPORTANCE OF ATTENDING COLLEGE

When one really evaluates the reason for attending college, it is merely about preparing yourself for a job and about the knowledge to carry out a profession. Students should go to college with the motivation and intentions of making a successful career in their chosen profession. You as a student will gain a wealth of knowledge which will allow you to succeed in future jobs, and even owning your own company.

Parents, teachers and counselors should encourage students to go to college. It's never too early to start talking to your children about college. Parents and teachers need to make children/students feel as though they have accomplished something and give them recognition.

Students tend to respond with interest and motivation to teachers who appear to be caring. Students should encourage each other to attend college.

One might ask what does a higher education provide for you. Simple answer. It provides a broader spectrum of opportunities for graduates versus those whom have not graduated from college. You also have greater promotion opportunities.

IS COLLEGE IMPORTANT TO YOU?

IF SO WHY?

REASONS WHY SOME STUDENTS GO TO COLLEGE

1. To impact future generations in their family.

2. To earn a degree.

3. To use an academic scholarship to pay for their education.

4. To use an athletic scholarship to get an education and at the same time be able to play the sport of your choice.

5. To have a better lifestyle.

6. College opens the door to opportunities.

EXCUSES FOR NOT ATTENDING COLLEGE

1. No one in my family ever went to college.

2. My grades are not good enough.

3. I can't afford to go to college.

4. I do not know how to apply or where to go.

5. College will be too hard for me, I'm not smart enough.

6. I'm not sure I will fit in or if I'll meet new friends.

7. My friends are not going to college.

8. I'm tired of school. I'd rather just get a job.

FAMILIARIZE YOURSELF WITH COMMUNITY COLLEGES VS. STATE/UNIVERSITY COLLEGES

Community College

1. 2 year colleges offer certificate programs and General education degrees (Associates of Arts Degree)

2. Technical programs/ Vocational Degrees

3. Transfer programs-AA or AS transferable for credit to a 4 year college.

Advantages:

Open enrollment, lower cost, 2 year degree can be accepted with a junior status at any 4 year school State wide.

Universities

Offers a Bachelor's Degree in 4 years, Master's Degree, Doctoral Degrees, and Professional Degrees MD.

Advantages:

1. Broader selection of majors and courses.

2. Name recognition.

3. Increased access to facility members who are more involved in researched and scholarly activities.

PARENTS SHOULD WANT THEIR CHILDREN TO HAVE A BETTER EDUCATION.

What Should High School Parents Do To Help Prepare Their Children For College?

1. Motivate them

2. Plant a seed for a better future

3. Start talking to your children about college at an early age

4. Connect/spend time with your children

5. Do activities you both love

6. Encourage your children

7. Communicate with your children

8. Keep tabs on what interest them and encourage them to pursue it

9. Talk to your children about sex, alcohol and drugs

10. Teach your children about goals/plans for the future

11. Parents should ask themselves is this what You want your child to do or is it what they want to do

PARENTS, KEEP A JOURNAL OF WAYS YOU COULD ENCOURAGE/HELP YOUR CHILD GRADUATE FROM HIGH SCHOOL AND PREPARE THEM FOR COLLEGE TO GET A HIGHER EDUCATION

What Should High School Students Do To Prepare Themselves For College?

1. Start thinking about college at an early age

2. Have dreams and visions

3. Set goals and have plans

4. Have good study habits/Make good grades

5. Take the ACT test and or the SAT test (if you are unsure take the practice test or the PSAT test)

6. Determine what you might study or major in at college

7. Gather a list of colleges you would like to attend. Go to each college website and gather information

8. Apply to the colleges of your choice/visit colleges

9. Apply for financial aid and scholarships

10. Make sure you take all your core courses

11. Be honest with your Parents about attending college. Don't go to college and waste your parent's money by flunking out or not attending classes. Don't mess up your scholarship if you receive one by not attending classes or by fooling around.

Students Should Write In Their Journal The Necessary Steps Needed To Prepare Themselves For College

Chapter 4

Being Recruited

THE RECRUITING PERIOD

The recruiting period can be a fun time, a nervous time, an exciting experience and sometimes it can be disappointing. There are certain times scouts and coaches can talk to you, visit you and offer you a scholarship. This is known as the "recruiting calendar." A lot can happen during this time. Some athletes will receive tons of recruiting letters, but not actually "get recruited." Some receive phone calls, but in time you will find out which coaches are really interested in you. Remember, you can be heavily recruited, but the recruiter can take one look at your grades and say, "NO WAY!" I can't stress enough how important it is to keep your grades up. The better your grades are, the more options you will have come the recruiting period.

There are many strategies that coaches and recruiters will use to get athletes into their programs. Sometimes athletes are just "tagalongs." Recruiters will appear to be interested in one athlete only to attract another. Athletes and their parents see the treatment of other athletes and are influenced by the obvious benefits. The results are sometimes "PACKAGE DEALS," where athletes are recruited in 2's, 3's, 4's, and even 5's. Whatever the tactics, don't be deceived by the recruiters' game playing.

Believe it or not, sometimes it doesn't work out for the athlete that is heavily recruited and the athlete who was less recruited gets an opportunity to play after all. There have been cases where, as a part of a deal, a coach will get hired so that his son or nephew can get recruited. None of these are good reasons to get recruited. Even though some aspects of recruiting may seem underhanded, there are honest coaches who will tell the student athlete that they are being offered a scholarship- but cannot promise that they will start or play much their freshman year.

♡ Make A List Off At Least Five Colleges You Are Interested In:

SELF PROMOTION

During the recruiting period there are many things you can do as a student athlete to increase your chances of success. You can email and call coaches, send letters to let them know who you are and that you are interested in attending that particular institution. Also, let them know why you think you deserve to be recruited. A coach cannot evaluate your athletic skills if he doesn't know you exist, right? You can be overlooked if you omit important information or if you do not apply to the college that is the right one for you. My advice to you is to take your time, know what you have to do, and do it correctly and in a timely manner. Follow the NCAA rules and guidelines, talk to the coaches and visit the campuses.

There are three basic, and effective ways to get on a coach's list as a possible recruit. Below is an example of a LETTER OF INTEREST and a PLAYER PROFILE (there's a version to fill out in the Prep to Pro Playbook in the back of the book) Use these along with a HIGHLIGHT VIDEO to get your name out there.

It's a good idea to make your own highlight film, even if your school makes it for you. You can add your own music and finishing touches to your own film. It can be a lot of fun and it will show you in the best light possible.

LETTER OF INTEREST

Date

Coach's Name
Address

Dear Coach_____, (It's good to personalize this and put the coach's actual name here.)

My name is_____. I am interested in attending (Name of School Here) and being a part of your team while I am there.

Now, list some of your academic and athletic accomplishments. Also list an upcoming schedule where this coach could possibly come and see you play.

Thank you for your time.

Sincerely,

You Name

Your Email

Your Phone Number

Your Parents Names and Phone Numbers

PLAYER PROFILE

[Top of the Page]

Your Name

Address, Email and Phone Number

Your High School and Graduation Year (Big and at the top. You want this to stand out at a glance.)

Your cumulative G.P.A. (That's the average of all the years you've been in high school up to that point... not just last quarter or year etc...)

Picture of you ATTACHED TO THE PAGE (Either printed on the page itself or stapled to the page so the two will not be separated.)

[Body of the Profile]

References

Academic and Athletic Accomplishments

Parents Names and Contact Information

DON'T FAKE THE NUMBERS

It's important that you do not lie about any of this information. Nothing will get you off a coach's list faster than inaccurate information. Coaches base their recruiting off of whether or not a prospective student athlete is eligible for admission into their school before anything else. If you say you have a 3.5 G.P.A but you really have a 3.3 that can be the difference between admission into that college or no chance at all. Once the coach knows the truth, you will be off their list. If they don't find out until you apply to the college, then you have just wasted their time and your time. If this is the case, you may find that you missed out on getting into a college and into an athletic program you really wanted to be in.

THINGS TO CONSIDER

You might want to think about the offensive or defensive scheme. If you play football for example, is it a PRO STYLE offense, easily transferable to the NFL? Does the defense run a 3-4 or 4-3 that's transferable to the NFL? Do they like run the ball or throw the ball? These questions may not matter to some players, but may be very important to others. Prep and high school coaches have some influence in helping an athlete to get recruited. If you have a coach who really cares, they will do what they can to help. They will put in a good word for you, make sure your paperwork is complete and correct and show concern about you furthering your education. Having a good relationship with your coach can be beneficial. But, you have to communicate with your coach and do your part to make it easy for the coach to help you.

NCAA RECRUITING RULES SUMMARY

NCAA Eligibility Center

Register with the Eligibility Center by completing an NCAA student release form during your junior year of high school. The guidance department or guidance counselor should have the necessary forms for the evaluation of your eligibility status. Registration has to be completed online. Visit NCAA clearinghouse.net.

CORRESPONDENCE

Correspondence begins September 1 of your junior year in high school.

Coaches or others at the university are permitted to send letters and printed materials such as faxes and e-mails.

PHONE CALLS

Phone calls may begin June 15 after completion of the junior year. A COACH or FACULTY MEMBER or OTHER ATHLETIC DEPARTMENT PERSONNEL are limited to one (1) phone call per week to the prospect or guardian(s). Exceptions may apply surrounding official visits, home visits and signing dates. PROSPECTS or GUARDIANS may call a coach as often as they wish. ENROLLLED collegiate student athletes may not make recruiting calls. You may telephone enrolled collegiate student athletes at your own expense. E-MAILS are UNLIMITED because they are not considered phone calls.

CONTACTS

(any face-to-face encounter during which dialogue occurs)

Contacts begin June 15 after the junior year. A college coach may contact a prospect or guardian(s) off campus. A coach MAY NOT contact a PROSPECT during competition. A coach MAY contact GUARDIANS during competition. Contacts are limited to 3 PER INSTITUTION.

OFFICIAL VISIT

Official visits are visits paid for by the institution you are visiting. You are allowed a total of 5 official visits to institutions. An official visit is limited to 48 hours.

UNOFFICIAL VISIT

Unofficial visits are visits you and your family pay for. You can show up at a college and check out the campus, meet the coach and generally do everything you need to check the school out. There is no limit to how many of these you may make or how long you can stay when visiting.

EVALUATIONS

Evaluations are any off-campus activity designed to assess athletics and or academics. DIVISION II INSTITUTIONS are not limited to the number of evaluations they may conduct.

VISITS/COLLEGE OPEN HOUSE DATES

Make sure you plan ahead. It's best to visit on a day when school is in session. If you are really interested in a particular school, set up an interview with the admissions office. Plan to take a tour of the campus. Visit classes, stay overnight and have a student show you around. This must be done through the admissions office. Attend an open house the college is offering. Some colleges offer FEE WAIVERS to families who attend their open house. Be sure to ask about this. If you are an athlete, you are allowed 5 official visits and unlimited unofficial visits. Contact the coaches and set up a meeting. If you are invited to a campus visit by a coach, they will arrange everything, including the completion of paperwork. All you have to do is show up.

INFORMATION TO GATHER

When you are considering a college and preparing for a visit, make sure you do your research. The Internet has made it much easier to find out information about colleges. Make sure you visit the school's website and gather information before you go on your trip. Here are some questions you should find out ahead of time, or ask on your visit.

- How does a freshman prepare for college?

- Are the freshmen assigned to counselors?

- What type of housing is available?

- What is the cost of housing?

- Is the housing area co-ed?

- How large are the classes?

- Do you have computer labs?

- Does the campus have a career office?

- How successful are graduating seniors in finding jobs in their areas of study?

While you are on your visit it is a good idea to sit in on a class or two and talk with the admissions counselors. Most often you will do most of this before having a sit down meeting with the coach. When you do meet the coach, it is important to BE PREPARED. Come with good questions.

IF YOU INTEND TO PLAY SPORTS

Here are a few more things to take into consideration:

- What is the distance from home?
- How many games or visits will your family be able to attend?
- Will you choose this college just to get away from home?
- What percentage of athletes graduate?
- How many students of your race or nationality graduate?
- What did you like about the visit?
- Did you like the coaches?
- Did you meet the office staff?
- Does the school ranking mean anything to you?
- Does the campus have dorms?
- Are they separate from the non-athlete dorms or housing?
- Is it a requirement for the athletes to stay in the dorms, and if so, how long?
- Do you have police escorts to home games?

QUESTIONS TO ASK A COACH DURING YOUR VISIT

- How does a freshman athlete prepare for the college level?
- What is your coaching philosophy?
- Where do you see me fitting into your system?
- Is your school "fully funded"?
- Would I have a chance to compete for a starting position?
- What is the off season program like?
- What does a week look like during the season?

QUESTIONS <u>NOT</u> TO ASK A COACH DURING YOUR VISIT

- Are you sponsored by NIKE?

- What will next year's uniforms looks like?

- Do you put names on the back of jerseys?

- Where will my locker be?

- Are cheerleaders at every game?

These are a few examples. Think about your concerns and ask questions. It is most important that parents and students take the time to BE PREPARED and make the most of your visits.

♡ Write In Your Journal About The Colleges You Have Visited Or The Schools You'd Like To Visit.

Another important factor in considering a college is who's already there. Take time to make an account of the roster. In other words, do your homework. Find out how many athletes are already playing in the same position. For example, if your position is QUARTERBACK, how many are in front of you—

- RSF (Red shirt Freshmen)

- TF/F (True Freshmen/Freshmen)

- SOP (Sophomore)

- JR (Junior)

- SR (Senior)

MY EXPERIENCE

When my son was being recruited, at the point where coaches were allowed to come to our home for a visit, it was a very exciting time for him and our family. As we were trying to decide which college he was going to attend, my family and I prayed and asked for God's guidance and help with making the right decision. We were able to use a process of elimination by listening and writing down everything that was told to us by each coach. We went over all of the information that was given to us by the coaches. From there we narrowed it down to three colleges. It was a tough decision.

My son and I compared notes. We based our decision on what was most important to our family. We took a lot of things into consideration. My son based his decision on things such as:

- The coach

- The school

- His major

- The type of offense they ran

- How far away he would be from home

- How many bowl games the school went to

- How many receivers were already ahead of him

Of course my reasons were a little different. I thought about what type of relationship my son and the coach would have. If he was going to be far away, how would I be assured that my son would be in good hands? What was the graduation rate among athletes, and not just athletes but African American football players? Another main reason for choosing the college I wanted my son to attend was the integrity of the coach.

Coach Fulmer, from the University of Tennessee, didn't once speak negative about the other two colleges. He didn't try to tear down the other colleges and he wished my son luck if he decided not to attend his university. I felt it was important to go with the coach with integrity. Although my son would be the one to make the final decision, he had his own reasons for choosing the college in which he attended. We felt he made the right choice.

YOUR POSITION

Keep in mind that sometimes the position you played in high school might change to a different position in college. A VERY IMPORTANT MESSAGE IS TO NOT LET YOUR FRIENDS OR TEAMMATES PERSUADE YOU TO SWITCH YOUR POSITION. They just might want the position, and this will provide the opportunity for them to move up, pushing you further back. So just do a good job in the position so you can move up. If you do change your position, make sure it is a decision made between you and the coach. Take a look and see what the team needs are. What's best for the team? For example, if a corner position is lacking and you are not being utilized at all, you might consider switching to corner. That's something to think about.

SCHOLARSHIPS

Athletic scholarships are one-year awards. That means that after the first year is up an award does not have to be renewed. If a student athlete doesn't perform on the football field, basketball court, baseball field or whatever their sport and their grades are not acceptable, the program is not obligated to provide the same award the following year. Athletic awards are agreed upon for one year at a time. Student athletes are always provided with a hearing if their aid is reduced or canceled. A representative from the institution's administration is present to make a final decision.

Don't think that because you have a scholarship award that it is automatically guaranteed for 4 or 5 years. That's why you have to continue to work hard on the field, on the court and in the classroom. All scholarships are not full rides. Some scholarships, such as track, are called "head count sports". NCAA baseball is classified as an "equivalency sport." That means that a coach can divide the 12 scholarships between a larger number of baseball players, giving 25 partials instead of 12 full scholarships. However, there is a possibility that a player can receive a "full ride," but that player has to have outstanding skills.

FULLY FUNDED

Not all colleges can offer the same amount of scholarships and there are limits, based upon the sport, to the amount of scholarships a coach has to hand out every year. It is false, that all athletes receive scholarships and that all scholarships are full scholarships. So take the time to find out how many scholarships a coach has to work with. For example, Division I NCAA football programs can offer 85 scholarships, where the same DI schools can offer 13 for basketball. However, if a school is not fully funded, they may only be able to offer 10 basketball scholarships.

VERBAL COMMITMENT

An athlete will sometimes make a verbal commitment to a coach because a scholarship is offered. Keep in mind that a verbal commitment is not binding and the athlete can change his or her mind at any time. I have known athletes to make verbal commitments before going on their five visits. They make a definite decision based on personal choice or because their friends have made a verbal commitment. Some of them are persuaded by their parents. Others may not want to attend that particular college or play for a certain coach, and when it's time to sign the letter of intent, the student signs with a different college. Students have that right.

I don't think parents should dictate where their child should attend college unless the parent is paying for their child to attend a particular college. I still feel like it should be up for discussion and hopefully the parent/parents and the child would come to an agreement in which both the child and the parent are comfortable with the decision. Be thankful that your parents are willing to spend THEIR OWN MONEY to provide a higher education for you.

If a student is offered a scholarship I still think it should be up for discussion, but I feel as though the student should have the final say so in this situation. If the student is offered more than one scholarship both the student and the parent should listen to each other's reasoning for attending or not attending a particular college. This is a very valuable life changing time in your lives so think carefully and make good decisions. Give the student an opportunity to make the choice but offer guidance along the way. Parents should make sure the student is satisfied with their decision. A coach may be disappointed when an athlete who verbally commits to them changes their mind, even becoming angry, but they will get over it. Other coaches will understand and wish the student well and move on.

STUDENTS SHOULD REMEMBER THAT IT'S NOT ALWAYS ABOUT GOING TO A SCHOOL JUST BECAUSE YOUR FRIENDS ARE GOING THERE. WHAT'S GOOD FOR THEM MAY NOT ALWAYS BE WHAT'S GOOD FOR YOU... AND WHAT'S GOOD FOR YOU... MAY NOT ALWAYS BE WHAT'S GOOD OR RIGHT FOR THEM.

Please keep that in mind because I've seen too many friends or classmates follow each other and for some reason or another it doesn't work out for one of you or two of you the way you thought it would or even hoped it would. So again... MAKE WISE DECISIONS!!!!!

♡ IT'S TIME TO ANALYZE AND DECIDE WHICH COLLEGE YOU WOULD LIKE TO ATTEND. EVALUATE YOUR PREVIOUS LIST OF COLLEGES AND THE SCHOOLS YOU HAVE VISITED AND/OR RESEARCHED.

PARENTS: TAKE TIME TO DISCUSS THE COLLEGES AND INFORMATION GATHERED ON YOUR STUDENT'S VISITS. TRY AND NARROW THAT LIST DOWN TO A TOP TWO OR THREE.

NLI (NATIONAL LETTER OF INTENT)

The National Letter of Intent is a letter or document a student athlete signs to commit to a participating NCAA college or university. When you sign a National Letter of Intent you agree to attend the college or university listed on the letter in exchange for that institution awarding an athletic scholarship or financial aid for one academic year. You also officially end the recruiting process and prevent other schools from contacting you. If you are under 21 years of age, you need a parent to sign the letter of intent to make it legally binding.

This is a critical time for students and parents. This can also be an exciting time for both. Parents may be happy that they won't have to pay for college; their child has decided to attend college to prepare for a productive life by earning a degree. Some parents never had an opportunity to go to college, but their child has been offered a scholarship, and that can be very emotional. Not only will their child get a good education, but they will also be able to play the sport of their choice. Signing your name on the National Letter of Intent is an honor and a great accomplishment.

TO THE PARENTS/GUARDIANS

At this stage, I know it is difficult to see your child grow up and go away to college. We buy them what they need to get started. We cry. We see how happy they are to leave home and we are joyful and sad at the same time. Sometimes moms have a more difficult time than the dads, because they don't want to "cut the cord," or they feel that they are losing the child. When children leave home, parents almost always know which ones will return to their hometown after they graduate and which ones will go elsewhere. Some parents are glad to see their children leave home, for it can be a sign of maturity. Whatever the case may be, our children grow up, and we hope they benefit from the lessons they learn at home, in the classrooms, in sports or wherever they go. WE WANT THEM TO MAKE GOOD CHOICES.

Chapter 5

College Student Athlete

ON YOUR OWN

Now that you are a college student and on your own, this is a big change for you and your parents. You have worked hard to get to where you are, you have plans and goals and you're all set. Children are almost always happy to get away from their parents, but little do they know, they might need their parents before their parents need them. When you go to college you're on your own. You won't have parents telling you what to do everyday, but you won't have them there to pick you up when you fall, to cook for you, clean for you, put gas in your car or cash in your hands.

Not every child is excited to leave home. Some kids have to be "pushed out of the nest" because they are afraid to leave home and others do not want to leave their parents home alone. Then there are children who think their parents will be there for every beckoned call, delivering money that grows on trees. When these kids don't have mommy and daddy around they might find out being on their own wasn't as fun as they thought.

Students sometimes experience tough times while away from home and actually learn to appreciate their parents more. Being on your own and being independent can lead to becoming more responsible. This will be reflected in your ability to keep up your grades and show respect for yourself and others. If you are having problems, talk to someone YOU CAN TRUST- a coach, an advisor or counselor; IT IS VERY IMPORTANT THAT YOU WORK CLOSELY WITH THEM.

If you received an athletic scholarship, don't let the coach, your teammates or your family down by not being able to play because of poor grades. Take advantage of everything offered to you. You have access to tutors, study hall and study groups, etc. It is also important that parents stay involved and communicate, even in college. You do not want to look up one day and see your child walking to the front door with bags in hand due to suspension or bad grades. Kids, make sure you leave home in good standing with your parents or guardians in case you do have to go back home. If you leave on a good note, you won't have a problem going back provided you are willing to abide by the rules. My advice is to stay focused and follow a plan so you won't have to return home before earning your degree.

NEW TECHNOLOGY

With all the new technology you might spend much more time on CELL PHONES, TEXTING, MYSPACE, FACEBOOK and TWITTER because you are on your own. Experiencing new freedom that was not granted by your parents can be an exciting proposition. It's important, however, that you are careful about sharing information on PERSONAL WEB PAGES. Your words and your pictures say a lot about you. You might be surprised to find out who looks at your web pages: employers, coaches, parents, teachers, family members and media – they all check it out. There have been many cases of student athletes being suspended or expelled for activities, photos and comments they have posted to their social networking pages.

ROOMMATES

It is not always good to have your friends as roommates for a long period of time. Being around each other too much can ruin a friendship. Often, even little things like, one of you being clean and the other messy, can cause a strain. Sometimes you may take advantage of a friend because you are on your own and feel that you can do whatever you want to do. You may not even realize that you are doing this because, after all, a good friend may not say anything about it. So remember to be considerate when rooming with anyone, even good friends. You wouldn't want to lose your friendship over silly things.

Whether you live with a friend or someone you don't know, you and your roommate should agree upon a set of rules. Rules establish expectations, guidelines and mutual respect. If your name is not on the lease, you should not be living there. Sometimes we want to help our friends by allowing them to stay with us, and the visit can turn into weeks and months. Keep in mind that YOU ARE RESPONSIBLE for whatever is broken or damaged. Also, if you are the friend who is allowed to stay with someone, step up to the plate and be responsible if you damage something, be courteous and find ways to contribute, like buying groceries and keeping the place clean.

When you move into a new place you should take pictures upon arrival and more when you move out, in case there are disagreements about who is responsible for damages, such as holes in the walls. Sometimes landlords promise to make repairs that are never done. Read the lease carefully, especially the FINE PRINT, because that's what it is and you have to "find the print." Make sure you have proof of the conditions when you move in and when you move out and keep record of your payments, requests and a general log of your time living there. This can save you a lot of hassle and money down the road.

CHOOSING YOUR CLASSES

Before you choose classes get a handbook listing the classes offered. This information should be available on your school's website, but if it's not, it will be available at the Registrar's Office. Stay focused so that your counselor or advisor won't give you incorrect information. YOU need to know FOR YOURSELF what general education classes you need to take, how many credits or units each one is worth, which classes count toward your major, which classes count toward general education credits. You might take a 3-unit class and pass it, but receive only one 1 credit for that particular class. DON'T BE AFRAID TO ASK QUESTIONS, ESPECIALLY IF YOU ARE AN ATHLETE.

You will need to keep track of your credits/units YOURSELF. It's important to work with an advisor WHO CARES and is willing to HELP you and WORK with you, but YOU have to be willing to work with them. If there is a hardship with you or someone in your immediate family that causes you to lack credits and become ineligible to play, a letter of appeal can be written to the NCAA stating the hardship or tragedy that occurred. Your Athletic Department will follow a protocol for this process. Players and parents WILL NOT be allowed to write the appeal. The NCAA will then determine your eligibility status.

It is also important that you know the sequence of classes. You do not want to take the most difficult classes for your major when easier ones should be taken first or during your sports season. Unfortunately, advisors and counselors may not always enroll students in classes in the recommended order.

Ask other students for recommendations of good instructors or professors for particular classes. The importance of staying focused about everything that concerns you cannot be stressed enough. YOU HAVE TO BE RESPONSIBLE for the classes you take and research the classes so you will know what they are about. Even if someone gives you a recommendation for a class, ask questions and use all of the resources available to you when making your decisions.

BE CAREFUL ABOUT SWITCHING MAJORS. IT COULD MAKE YOU INELIGIBLE TO PLAY A SPORT BECAUSE YOU WILL NOT RECEIVE CREDIT FOR SOME CLASSES YOU TOOK PRIOR TO CHANGING YOUR MAJOR, EVEN IF YOU PASSED THOSE CLASSES. YOU WILL NOT ALWAYS BE INFORMED, SO FIND OUT THE CONSEQUENCES OF CHANGING A MAJOR. Seriously think before changing your major. Again, ask all the important questions about graduation requirements and credits.

NCAA ELIGIBILITY REGULATIONS

The NCAA requires that you sign two forms, the NCAA Student Athlete Statement and the NCAA Drug Testing Consent Form:

- NCAA Student-Athlete Statement includes 4 parts:

    i. Eligibility- You affirm to the best of your knowledge that you are eligible to compete in intercollegiate competition.

    ii. Buckley Amendment Consent- You consent to this institution only, its athletics conference (if any) and the NCAA to disclose the following documents: the student athletic eligibility form; the results of the NCAA drug test and any and all transcripts from your high school, this institution or any junior college or 4-year institutions you attended; pre-college test scores; records regarding your financial aid and any papers or information pertaining to your NCAA eligibility

    iii. Incoming Freshmen-Affirmation or Affirmation of ACT or SAT Score

    iv. Result of Drug Test

- NCAA Drug Testing Consent Form

You are affirming that you are aware of the NCAA drug testing program and you are agreeing to allow NCAA to test you in relation to any participation by you in any NCAA championship or in any post season game certified by the NCAA for the banned drugs listed in Bylaw 31.2.3.1. Also if you participate in Division I football or track and field, you are agreeing to be tested on a year-round basis for anabolic agents, diuretics and urine manipulators.

Keep in mind that every year the NCAA publishes a SUMMARY OF THE NCAA REGULATIONS. There are also many specific requirements that must be met during the recruitment process to ensure initial eligibility. You may REVIEW the student athlete statement BEFORE you sign it. You may obtain a summary from the Director of Athletics.

KNOW THE NCAA RULES

Every year thousands of college athletes participate in NCAA regulated sports. With just a small mistake or even a misunderstanding of the NCAA rules, a college athlete's career can come to an end. It is very important for the athlete and their parents to know and understand the NCAA rules. Not only are the recruiting rules, and the admission standards important, but it is also VERY IMPORTANT to understand IMPROPER BENEFITS.

Improper Benefits are considered anything that rewards an athlete for playing at a college. Some coaches may give improper benefits to get a student athlete to participate at their college. Sometimes school boosters try to give gifts and some agents will try to give a student athlete or parents a lot of money, pay their rent, buy expensive gifts, or cars to try to get the student athlete to leave school early. Agents will sometimes do some of those things so that they can hurry up and get paid.

AGAIN!!! KNOW THE NCAA RULES regarding ILLEGAL BENEFITS and IMPROPER BENEFITS.

Every single year you hear about an athlete , coach, or a school in trouble, and scholarships being taken away merely because they violated NCAA rules. So be very careful if you or a family member is offered anything for free or at a discount because it could very well be a violation. Needless to say, sometimes an athlete or a family member will except benefits from someone and everything is A-OK until things don't go the agent's way, a booster's way, or maybe even things don't go the way a coach wants it to go. Maybe it doesn't go the way the athlete wants it to go or the way a family member thinks/wants it to go. What happens then? Someone gets upset or unhappy about something and reports it to the NCAA, or someone will tell another person and that person tells someone else and before you know it, it's all on the news or in the news paper

The NCAA has a lot of rules that govern/dictates what student athletes may and may not do on and off the playing field. If you are a relative of a student athlete please be advised that there are NCAA rules that pertain to you also.

PARENTS MUST KNOW AND UNDERSTAND THE NCAA RULES:

Even parents have to abide by the NCAA rules as well as the athlete. Parents can't accept gifts from boosters, agents, coaches, schools or anyone.

Parents of athletes can't make bets on their son or daughter and make money.

Parents cannot get a special discount at a hotel when they come to visit their child just because they are the parents of a student athlete.

Parents are not permitted to ride on the team bus.

Anyone who supports a collegiate athletics program becomes a (RAI) Representatives of Athletics Interest, better known as a booster.

Sports wagering is prohibited by the NCAA. The minute you make a bet on any college or professional sport , or gives information to someone who gambles, you are declared ineligible to compete in college sports.

If you accept or place a bet on any college or professional team other than your own you will be suspended automatically for one year. If you accept or make a bet on any team at your school you will become permanently ineligible. You also run the risk of being arrested and charged with a crime because sports wagering is illegal in every state except Nevada, but even in Nevada it is against NCAA rules for a student athlete to make any type of wager on a sports event. Sports bribery is illegal in every state.

The student athlete should also be very careful who they hang out with and be careful of the places you go. You don't want to get into any fights or confrontations, especially when someone gets hurt or injured. You don't want to ever put yourself in a position where you are knowingly in the wrong place at the wrong time. In other words, you know you shouldn't be going somewhere but yet you still go because your buddies are going.

Again, relatives nor friends can except benefits from an agent , financial advisor, or any one else associated with an agency business. Benefits include, transportation, money, and gifts but not limited to just these. It doesn't matter the value of the benefit or whether it was used. It's the f that you accepted the gift or gifts.

It's alright for parents to give their own child gifts and goodies. It's a good thing because if that wasn't so, then I'd say that they were really going overboard with the rules.

The NCAA rules are clear so if you are unsure of whether something is a benefit or not, you should contact the compliance office at your particular institute or college for more information. It's always better to be safe than sorry.

If a student athlete is found in violation of NCAA rules, often times the student athletes and their families are required to repay the amount of money or equivalent if it was a service. If the benefit is more than $100.00 the student athlete becomes ineligible until the NCAA reinstates them. This process takes time so the athlete may sometimes miss competing in games. Even if the athlete gets reinstated they could still miss some games. If you don't agree with the decision the NCAA made you have the right to an appeal.

SOME IMPORTANT THINGS TO REMEMBER:

In any sport, an athlete's scholarship will normally terminate if the student signs a professional contract.

In a sport you become ineligible if you have agreed orally or in writing to be represented by an agent for marketing your athletic ability or reputation in that sport.

You need to know that there are many restrictions and consequences concerning substance abuse for each one of the professional leagues.

Your financial aid could get cancelled by your institution if you reach an agreement with an agent.

PLEASE NOTE THAT: In the sport of basketball the athlete may enter a professional league's draft without jeopardizing eligibility in that sport, as long as you are not drafted and you've declared in writing to your institute/college director of athletics your intention to resume intercollegiate basketball participation within 30 days after the draft.

There are so many NCAA rules and by laws. You just have to know them for yourself. Again, it's always better to be safe than sorry. If you are unsure about any information regarding any NCAA rules, you should contact the compliance office at your institute/college.

Some schools get paid a lot of money from the games played at their schools by these athletes. Some of these athletes, a family member of an athlete or a school have previously violated some of the NCAA rules, and 2 years or more have passed since the athlete has graduated or left the school. The NCAA will still have to investigate to find out what occurred.

Hopefully one day soon the NCAA will re-evaluate some of their rules and pay the student athlete for playing the sport of their choice. Maybe if that happens there will be less violations.

ADDITIONAL NCAA RULES FOR THE UPCOMING YEARS (2012-2015)

PLEASE KEEP IN MIND THAT THE NCAA RULES CONSTANTLY CHANGE. REFER TO THEIR WEB PAGE ON A REGULAR BASIS FOR UPDATES.

STIPEND PAYMENTS

In October 2011, the NCAA Division 1 Board of Directors approved a $2,000 annual stipend that would give student athletes with full scholarships extra spending money to use for extra expenses needed beyond tuition, room and board, and fees.Complaints started pouring in and by late December 2011, 160 schools had signed to override legislation to force a suspension of the rule.

There has been a lot of talk about the stipend regarding NCAA rules, how it would apply to women's athletes and sports with partial scholarships. There was also some concern about when it would go into effect and how would the student athlete spend the extra money. It seems as though some of the larger schools were for it while some of the smaller schools were against it due to budget reasons and whatever other reasons they were concerned about.

A new stipend proposal will have another vote in April. If it passes it would go back to the membership for another 60 day comment period.

In my opinion, the additional scholarship money would be a big help to our students. It would allow each student to have extra spending money. On the other hand I also feel that all students should have a course in money management so that they will know how to manage their money better if and when they do get extra.

Student athletes who signed a letter of intent in November 2011, and who were promised additional money will get it.

MULTIYEAR SCHOLARSHIP

Individual schools can choose to award multiyear scholarships to student athletes if they desire to do so. With the new rule a scholarship can be guaranteed for the player's entire career and would be unable to revoke it based on an athlete's performance. No longer can a coach pull an existing player's scholarship and offer it to another recruit they feel has more athletic potential. Keep in mind that with the new rule a scholarship could still be pulled for reasons such as poor grades, academic misconduct or other forms of improper behavior.

Under the current model athletic scholarships are renewable every year and can be revoked for any reason.

There was also talk that the NCAA is thinking about limiting the number of scholarships from 85 to 80 for football and 15 to 13 for basketball. The board has rejected limiting the scholarships so it will stay as is for now.

STRICTER STANDARDS FOR HIGH SCHOOL STUDENTS AND FOR JUNIOR COLLEGE STUDENT TRANFERS

High school students ENROLLING in AUGUST 2015 have to complete 10 of the 16 total core courses BEFORE THE START OF THEIR SENIOR YEAR.

7 of the 10 must be in English, math and science. Eligibility requirements increased from 2.0 GPA to 2.3 for incoming freshmen.

The NCAA will require STUDENT ATHLETES coming from a Community College or Junior College, transfering to a State or University, they must have a 2.5 GPA up from 2.0 to be eligible for competition.

Those who didn't meet the mark upon high school graduation must complete a core curriculum that includes English, math, and science.

The board also voted to create an ACADEMIC REDSHIRT YEAR, in which athletes who underperform coming out of high school can still receive a scholarship and practice with their teams, but can't travel or participate in games. In other words, if a student athlete meets the 2.0 GPA requirement but falls short of the 2.3 GPA required for competition, the NCAA approved a proposal that will allow the student athlete to remain on scholarship for the year.

POST SEASON RULES

To help improve the graduation rate, the Academic Progress Rate (APR) cutline will increase from the current 900 to 930 in four years, which is about a 50 percent graduation rate. Schools that fail to reach that standard will be ineligible for NCAA post season play, including bowl games, championship games and basketball tournaments.

Harsher penalties will be imposed on the teams that underperform in the classroom. Teams that miss the cutline might have to replace some hours of weekly practice with academic studies and probably reduce their number of games. For the most severe cases, there could also be coaching suspensions and financial aid reductions.

For 24 months beginning in the next academic year, teams must make the current 900 APR each year or a 930 average over the same time frame to be eligible for post season play.

The new requirements will take effect beginning in the fall of 2012 and will have a two year implementation before the benchmark moves from 900 to 930.

To compete in post season games in 2012-2013 and 2013-2014, teams must have scored 930 during the two most recent years

In 2014-2015 teams that don't achieve a 930 four year APR or a 940 average for the most recent two years will be ineligible for post season games.

FYI: If this rule had gone into effect last school year it would of kept probably about 7 of the 68 team NCAA men's basketball out of tournaments and it would have prevented about 8 of the 70 football teams probably from competing in bowl games.

I hope now that students will take their work in the classrooms more seriously and realize that school comes first and sports come second. I also hope that the student will realize how important it is to get a good education and earn a degree .

BASKETBALL RECRUITING

A new recruiting model for basketball will be in place by August 1, 2012. The NEW RULES will ALLOW COACHES to make unlimited calls or send unlimited texts to prep recruits after June 15 of their sophomore year.

The changes were made to encourage coaches to get to know the recruits and their families on a more personal level.

The recruiting calendar will also ALLOW COACHES FOUR evaluation days in APRIL (which was previously considered to be a dead period). But in JULY they will go FROM 20 ALLOWABLE DAYS TO 12.

Official visits can begin on JANUARY 1 of a prospect's JUNIOR YEAR with the school paying for the travel expenses for the student and a parent effective August 1, 2012.

Some contact will be allowed at a prospect's school during the prospect's junior year in conjunction with an evaluation.

Staged, on- campus evaluations will be permitted on a recruiting visit.

THE NEW RECRUITING MODEL FOR BASKETBALL WILL BE IN PLACE BY AUGUST I, 2012.

IF THERE IS NO EFFECTIVE DATE OR A DATE TO BE IMPLEMENTED, LISTED ABOVE REGARDING THE NEW NCAA RULES, PLEASE CHECK WITH THE NCAA OR YOUR ATHLETIC DEPARTMENT FOR SPECIFIC DATES. YOU MAY ALSO GO ONLINE TO GET THIS INFORMATION.

PLEASE FEEL FREE TO GO ONLINE ANYTIME YOU OR YOUR PARENTS NEED CLARIFICATION ABOUT ANY NCAA RULES.

STUDENTS/PARENTS:

DO YOU HAVE ANY QUESTIONS/CONCERNS REGARDING THE NCAA RULES?

DO YOU UNDERSTAND THE NCAA RULES?

REDSHIRTING

Redshirt is a term used with American college athletics referring to the delaying or suspending of an athlete's participation to lengthen his or her period of eligibility.

In a given sport a student's eligibility is four years. It usually takes four years of academic classes to obtain a bachelor's degree. If a student athlete chooses to redshirt for one year, then that would allow the student eligibility for 5 years. In other words, they could spread the 4 years over a 5 year period. The athlete would attend classes at the college or university and practice with the team but may not play in games if they were redshirting.

Here are a few reasons why a student athlete might choose to redshirt:

- To add size

- To physically mature

- To learn the team's play book

- To be cleared by NCAA clearinghouse

- Because a coach gives them that status

- To wait until a position is open for a freshman

- To gain a year of participation with the team prior to participation

MEDICAL REDSHIRT

This is a term used to replace a season lost completely or almost completely to injury in which a student will gain an extra year instead of just having four academic years.

GRAYSHIRT

If an injury occurs right before college and you need a year to recuperate, the grayshirt student can attend school but can't enroll as a full time student, nor will the student receive a scholarship that year. The student is not an official member of the team, does not participate in practices or games, nor receive financial assistance from their athletic department. The student can attend school as a part-time regular student and can later join the team.

Keep In Mind That Just Because A Coach Has Given Redshirt Status To An Athlete At The Beginning Of The Year, It Is Not Confirmed Until The End Of The Season.

A player can still be eligible to participate especially if a player shows great talent, or if injuries occur, a coach can remove the redshirt status and allow the player to participate for the remainder of that year.

PLEASE BE CAREFUL ABOUT MAKING A DECISION TO COME OUT OF REDSHIRTING STATUS AT THE END OF THE YEAR. If a player participates in only one game or even one play, the redshirt status will COUNT as an eligible season. If your coach wants to redshirt you your freshman year, it's not always a bad idea. Some of the best athletes have a redshirt tag on them. It's an opportunity to learn and better prepare to play the next year. You can learn a lot by just watching!

REDSHIRT FRESHMAN

This is an academic sophomore in his second year but first season of athletic eligibility.

TRUE FRESHMAN

This is a first year student who has practiced and participated with the team.

TRAVELING WITH THE TEAM

Not everyone will have the opportunity to travel with the team to away games. You really have to work hard to earn a spot on the travel squad. There might be some players who have out-performed you, or are next in line who will get to travel with the team. Don't get discouraged. It can be very difficult sitting at home, in your dorm room or apartment while your roommates/teammates are on the road with the team. You might be all alone watching the team on T.V. Keep your head up. Stay encouraged. Work harder. Stay focused on what you need to do to advance to the top. Your time will come.

What if you travel with the team and don't get any playing time? Instead of feeling useless, this time could be used as a learning experience to remind you to do the best you can when your opportunity comes. Coaches want to see consistency, not just flashes of brilliance. Another player might out-perform you, take your spot and move up, but stay prepared. If an injury or anything unexpected occurs you must be prepared to play at any given moment.

If you are not playing with the team due to low grades ask your counselor or advisor to discuss them with you. Be sure you have a clear understanding of why you are ineligible so you can take the appropriate actions to become eligible.

♡ Take Time To Write On Paper What You Need To Do To Improve In The Classroom And On The Field. This Is A Time To Make An Assessment Of Yourself, And Then Make Appropriate Changes

DISAPPOINTMENTS

When you were recruited some of the coaches came to your home, looked your parents and you in the eyes, and expressed their desire to have you play for their school. At that time everyone was excited and happy. Later, your parents fill up their gas tanks, or they get on an airplane, using their last few dollars to see you play your first game. They watch for you every quarter and don't see you, or they blink once and you are off the field.

If this happens to you it's best to talk to the coach and see if the issue or issues can be resolved. First, make sure you have done all the right things before you point fingers at anyone. Then respectfully, you (and your parents, if they wish) express your concerns to the coach. Parents should listen to both sides. After all, there are two sides to every story. And if you are disappointed because your parents aren't supportive, find out what the problem is. It might be something beyond their control. Stay strong and encourage yourself to stay motivated. Some players will have to wait longer than others to play, but it's also important to know where you stand in order to improve. Continue to work hard at practice and in the classroom. Good things come to those who wait, and if you have to wait, realize that your time will come.

♡ HAVE YOU HAD ANY DISAPPOINTMENTS?

♡ HOW DID YOU DEAL WITH THOSE CHALLENGES?

TRANSFERRING

You might get upset because you don't think you are getting enough playing time, no playing time at all or the coach who recruited you has accepted another job. One day you may decide to transfer to a different college.

According to the NCAA rules, you will have to sit out for one season before you are allowed to participate at the new college, unless you transfer into a Division III program. However, I have known of a case in basketball where a Division I athlete did not have to sit out. You need to do your homework to see what colleges will accept you and what transfer rules will apply. YOU HAVE TO GET WRITTEN PERMISSION FROM THE NCAA before you or your parents can talk to any coaches. If you do decide to transfer you will still have to prove yourself worthy of getting a spot on the team, and it doesn't always mean that you will automatically earn a spot as a starter.

CHOOSING TO LEAVE SCHOOL EARLY

An athlete might choose to leave school early for several different reasons. They might feel strongly about their decision. Here are a few reasons why an athlete MIGHT consider leaving college after their junior year rather than choosing to finish school:

- They may feel that they are good enough to play at the next level right now.

- Pressure from family members

- Finance problems

- Family issues (maybe a family member is sick)

- Peer Pressure

- They are tired of school

- They've completed their courses and can graduate early.

As long as you've completed 3 years of school after graduating from high school, you may enter the NFL draft. Be sure to check your advisory board and NCAA rules regarding this issue. The NFL has a college advisory committee and you can now request information regarding your potential draft status without jeopardizing your eligibility. You will have to sign a notarized petition for special eligibility with the NFL.

If you are a football player contemplating leaving college early make sure you PROTECT YOUR ELIBILITY WHILE YOU TEST THE WATERS. If you have any questions contact:

NFL College Advisory Committee

Attention: Player Personnel Dept. National Football League

280 Park Avenue

New York, New York 10017

Phone number: 212-450-2215

Conclusion

As I was writing my books, I wanted the information I shared to be perceived as coming from a Mother speaking to her children and wanting them to know that I care about them. It is my desire that you have been inspired by reading my books and I hope that you got a lot of much needed information out of the books. I want the best for our children. I felt that if I could help motivate the students to stay in school and get an education, and to pass on to them some valuable information that I've learned, then that would make me happy. I want them to start thinking about their future at an early age. I want them to be successful.

I've seen too many talented children give up on their dreams because someone told them that they couldn't do it or because they didn't think they could, or they nor their parents knew where to began.

I wanted to also share information with parents. I wanted the parents to get more involved with their children and share information with them also and not just their children. Some of the information was maybe something they never thought about looking into or maybe never had to deal with.

Whenever I was getting ready to deal with another adult, I always wanted to be or at least appear to be prepared in knowing what I was talking about so that I could be on the same level as the person I was dealing with. That's what I want to do for the parents. My point was to make them get involved or feel more involved with their children. I put myself in their position. I wanted the parents to get the same thing I was concerned about receiving and that was knowledge and information.

All this inspired me to write these two books "From Prep" and "To Pro". Both of these books are Through the Eyes of a NFL Mom.

Part 2:
PLAYBOOK

From Prep Playbook

PLAYER PROFILE

HIGH SCHOOL: _____

GRADUATION
YEAR: _____

Your Name: _____

Address: _____

_____

_____

Email: _____

Phone Number: _____

Cumulative G.P.A. _____

BODY OF THE PROFILE

References: _____

_____

_____

_____

_____

_____

_____

_____

**Academic and
Athletic
Accomplishments:** _____

_____

_____

_____

_____

_____

_____

_____

_____

**Parents' Names
and Contact
Information:** _____

_____

_____

Picture of you ATTACHED TO THE PAGE (Either printed on the
page itself or stapled to the page so the two will not be separated.)

❤ WHAT ARE YOUR DREAMS AND VISIONS?

_____

_____

_____

_____

_____

_____

_____

_____

_____

_____

_____

_____

_____

♡ DO YOU NEED TO BRING YOUR GRADES UP?

_____

♡ HOW WILL YOU DO IT?

SOME OPTIONS ARE TO:

- Try harder
- Repeat the class
- Do extra credit
- How about summer school
- Find out if after school classes are offered

_____

_____

_____

_____

_____

_____

_____

DO YOU HAVE ATTITUDES THAT NEED ADJUSTING? BE SPECIFIC:

_____

_____

_____

_____

_____

_____

_____

_____

_____

_____

_____

_____

_____

_____

PARENTS, DO YOU NEED TO MAKE ADJUSTMENTS TO HELP YOUR CHILD?

_____

_____

_____

_____

_____

_____

♡ WHAT DO YOU SEE AS YOUR GOOD CHALLENGES?

_____

_____

_____

_____

_____

_____

♡ WHAT DO YOU SEE AS YOUR BAD CHALLENGES?

_____

_____

_____

_____

_____

_____

♡ WHAT PEER PRESSURES DO YOU FACE?

_____

_____

_____

_____

_____

_____

_____

_____

♥ PLANNING AHEAD

WHERE DO YOU SEE YOURSELF IN THE NEXT 5 TO 10 YEARS?

_____

_____

_____

_____

_____

_____

_____

_____

_____

_____

_____

_____

ARE YOU LOOKING AHEAD, OR ARE YOU JUST
PLANNING FOR THE NEXT 24 HOURS?

_____

_____

_____

DO YOU PLAN TO ATTEND COLLEGE?

_____

IF SO, WHAT ACCOMPLISHMENTS DO YOU WANT TO
MAKE?

_____

_____

_____

_____

_____

_____

_____

_____

_____

_____

WHAT DO YOU NEED TO DO IN HIGH SCHOOL TO GET TO COLLEGE?

_____

_____

_____

_____

_____

_____

_____

_____

_____

_____

_____

DO YOU WANT TO GO TO COLLEGE JUST TO PLAY SPORTS?

_____

_____

_____

DO YOU WANT TO PLAY HIGH SCHOOL SPORTS MORE THAN YOU WANT TO GET GOOD GRADES?

_____

_____

_____

_____

♡ TAKE A MOMENT AND WRITE DOWN YOUR GOALS:

YOUR GOALS MIGHT BE TO:

- Get better grades now in high school
- Take the proficiency exam and pass it
- Take the exit exam and pass it
- Do well in a chosen sport
- Graduate from high school
- Graduate from college with a degree
- Play in a professional sport

PLAYBOOK

EXERCISE

Just in case you don't know where to begin or you don't know what your dreams are, just take a few moments and do this exercise: Go into a quiet room, close your eyes and visualize on what you want to do in life. What would you like to be doing 5 years from now? 10 years from now? Wait a minute and keep your eyes closed. If closing your eyes doesn't work for you, or if it's not cool, then just sit in that quiet place and think for a minute. We're not done yet. Don't give up so easy. Concentrate until you can see it. OK, that's good. Now, did you see how easy that was? If you participated in this exercise, thank you. You did a GREAT JOB!

♡ WHAT DID YOU SEE?

_____

_____

_____

_____

_____

_____

_____

_____

♡ HOW DID IT FEEL WHEN YOU WERE VISUALIZING YOUR FUTURE?

_____

_____

_____

_____

_____

_____

_____

_____

_____

_____

_____

_____

_____

The Mathematics of Success

GOALS	=	PLANS
PLANS	=	ACTIONS
ACTIONS	=	ACHIEVEMENTS
ACHIEVEMENTS	=	RESULTS
RESULTS	=	SATISFACTION
SATISFACTION	=	ME

♡ WRITE DOWN YOUR FORMULA FOR SUCCESS:

PICK ONE GOAL, THEN WRITE DOWN THE RESULT YOU WANT, THE PLAN/ACTIONS NECESSARY TO GET THAT RESULT AND THE SATISFACTION YOU WANT IN ACCOMPLISHING YOUR GOAL.

_____

_____

_____

_____

_____

_____

_____

PLAYBOOK

♡ WHAT ARE YOUR REASONS FOR ATTENDING, OR WANTING TO ATTEND, COLLEGE?

_____

_____

_____

_____

_____

♡ MAKE A LIST OF AT LEAST 5 COLLEGES YOU ARE INTERESTED IN.

_____

_____

_____

_____

_____

_____

_____

♡ WRITE IN YOUR JOURNAL ABOUT THE COLLEGES YOU
HAVE VISITED OR THE SCHOOLS YOU'D LIKE TO
VISIT:

_____

_____

_____

_____

_____

_____

_____

_____

_____

_____

_____

_____

_____

_____

♡ It's Time To Analyze And Decide Which College You Would Like To Attend. Evaluate Your Previous List Of Colleges And The Schools You Have Visited And/Or Researched.

_____

_____

_____

_____

_____

_____

_____

_____

_____

_____

_____

_____

PARENTS: Take Time To Discuss The Colleges And Information Gathered On Your Student's Visits.

♡ TRY AND NARROW THAT LIST DOWN TO A TOP TWO OR THREE.

_____

_____

_____

♡ TAKE TIME TO WRITE ON PAPER WHAT YOU NEED TO DO TO IMPROVE IN THE CLASSROOM AND ON THE FIELD. THIS IS A TIME TO MAKE AN ASSESSMENT OF YOURSELF, AND THEN MAKE APPROPRIATE CHANGES.

_____

_____

_____

_____

_____

_____

_____

♡ HAVE YOU HAD ANY DISAPPOINTMENTS?

_____

_____

_____

_____

_____

_____

_____

_____

_____

_____

_____

_____

_____

_____

_____

♡ HOW DID YOU DEAL WITH THOSE CHALLENGES?

_____

_____

_____

_____

_____

_____

_____

_____

_____

_____

_____

_____

_____

_____

_____

PLAYBOOK

Journal

_____

_____

_____

_____

_____

_____

_____

_____

_____

_____

_____